# Carlson/Engblom/Westling Family History

# Carlson/Engblom/Westling Family History

Dr. Gail Carlson Fail

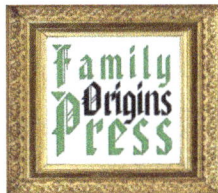

Family Origins Press

ISBN: 978-0-9888632-9-3
Library of Congress Control Number: 2015942045


Manufactured in the United States

Family Origins Press
An Imprint of Ink Brush Press

Austin, Texas

For all my Swedish family members,
past, present, and future

# Carlson/Engblom/Westling
# Family History

My mother's immediate family was Swedish except for her short, muscular half-Finnish grandfather, Anders. It was a bit of a scandal at the time he married my tall Swedish great grandmother Lotten. However, Anders was generally accepted by the 19th century, central Texas Swedish community because his mother was Swedish, he spoke Swedish, he took a Swedish last name, and he was a staunch Lutheran. Also, he managed to make a lot of money, which never hurts a man's social position. After a few generations, the stigma of a Finnish relative has passed away and now seems a bit silly.

My Scandinavian forbears came to the central Texas hill country near the capitol city of Austin in the 1880s, only about fifty years after the first European settlers arrived there. They arrived when Texas was still a frontier state. I grew up hearing stories about the Carlson and Westling families, the storybook romance between my great grandmother Lotten Westling and her husband Anders Engblom, and their lives in nineteenth century Sweden and Texas.

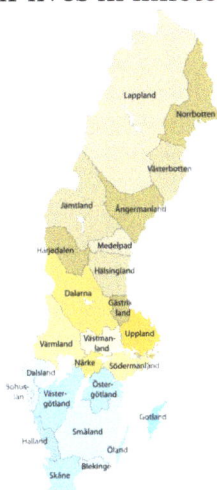

Swedish
traditional
provinces

Sweden has 25 traditional and cultural areas called provinces, once managed by separate rulers. In modern times government administration is by county, but in many cases county lines have followed those of the old provinces. My Carlson relatives were born in the southern provinces of Östergötland and Småland. Most of the Texas Swedes were from Småland.

Each province has a slightly different Swedish dialect. Some of the rural dialects are so localized that linguists call them "parish speech" (sockenmål). The Carlsons and Westlings spoke the more widely used dialect called Götaland, which was common all over Southern Sweden. But people from Östergötland and Småland still had slightly different accents.

Mama always had the attitude that Texas Swedes were a superior group of people, and was extremely proud of her heritage. Having a half-Finn in the group didn't seem to bother her much, especially since his other half was Swedish. Also, she very much loved and admired her grandfather Anders. Mama's father Oscar Carlson claimed that Swedes in general were higher quality folks than other Europeans or Americans. Papa, whose ancestry was a mixed bag of English, Native American, German and who-knows-what, thought this was snooty nonsense. I suspect Papa was right. I find all my ancestors interesting, Swedish or not.

I am the youngest daughter of Gorman Andrew Craven (the mixed bag) and Charlotte Rosebell Carlson (the almost-pure Swede). My parents had four children: Susan King, Carl Craven, Jerry Craven, and me, Gail Fail. All of us are retired now and our parents are dead. Sue and Jerry live in opposite ends of Texas, Carl is in Arizona, and I am in California.

Around January 2012 I began collating our old family documents, pictures and stories in order to write up our family history and a bit about the accompanying world, national and local events that influenced our ancestors' lives. My siblings and I each remember different family stories, and it has been fun compiling and comparing our recollections. I am writing this for my family, and especially for the younger ones, who may at some point find their ethnic and genetic heritages worthy of notice. I have focused on the Carlson family, but included some information on the Westlings and Anders Engblom. I have not included much detail on the members of my own generation, or our children and grandchildren. I have written mostly about the Carlsons and some about the Engbloms and the Westlings as well.

My Mama was the only child of Oscar Carlson and Ella Engblom. They named her Charlotte after Ella's mother, but I am not sure where Rosebell came from. It means "beautiful rose." Mama's relatives did not use her first name, and I never even knew she had one until I was a teenager. All the Swedes called her "Rosabell" or "Bell."

Mama knew a few words in Swedish, but was not fluent. She maintained a few Swedish habits. One was a love, or maybe an addiction, for strong coffee. She made really good Swedish meatballs, fruit soup and rice pudding, dishes that her father enjoyed. She wisely never served the kids lutefisk but she bought pickled herring for her dad.

The Westlings, Carlsons and Anders Engblom arrived in Texas speaking little or no English. The younger ones learned English quickly, but the elders still spoke Swedish at home their entire lives. Swedish language summer classes were common throughout the Swedish settlements, so the children could maintain fluency.

There was a fair amount of Swenglish spoken, after a few years in America. This was the use of English with a Swedish cadence and rhythm. Swenglish also included the changing of English words to a more Swedish pronunciation. For example, a creek was a "kricka."

The older Swedish immigrants to Texas ate Swedish-style meals, and worshipped at a Lutheran Church with services in Swedish. Their children mainly married other Texas Swedes, but many of their grandchildren (like my Mama) married outside the Swedish community and spoke little if any Swedish.

Among Swedish Texans, the resistance to losing the old country language, food and other customs was a bit stronger than among Swedes elsewhere in America.

There is an illustrative story published in *American Swedish 73*, about Texas Swedes and their desire to keep their native language in church. An older Swedish woman asked her Lutheran pastor, "Is it necessary that we have that Yankee language in our church?"

The pastor replied, "There have been some requests from the younger members, and furthermore, God understands that language also."

The woman said, "I am sure He does, but He does not like it."

My grandfather Oscar's immigrant parents were Carl August Carlson and Matilda Persson. His older siblings were Verner, Annie, Arvid, Jennie, Ellen, and Richard. Oscar was the first one to be born in Texas. Two other children, Erik and Nina, were born after Oscar. Both of them died young.

Grandmother Ella's parents were Anders Engblom and Lotten Westling, both immigrants. Ella was the oldest of four, all born in Texas. Two of her brothers were Theodore and Rudolph, and the third brother died as a toddler. I don't know his name.

If you get confused while reading this, and forget how someone fits into the family, I have included a summary of the lineage for each family (for three generations), at the end.

Mama gave me a stack of old Carlson, Westling and Engblom family photos and papers in the 1970s. She and her father had kept them in various boxes over the years, and some had been folded, scribbled on, scratched and chewed by roaches (a ubiquitous problem in southeast Texas). I put them into an album, and typed up notes on what she could remember of her family. When I started doing online research on Carlson genealogy, I located a couple of Carlson cousins and set up a meeting with them in Texas. Foolishly, I set up the meeting for August, a particularly warm time of year in central Texas.

4

However, the timing allowed me to meet my newly located relatives, to see some of my same-old relatives, and to attend a huge science fiction convention in San Antonio. That city is handily close to the homes of some of the Carlson cousins. My sister Sue, her daughter Beth and I drove to San Antonio from Sue's home in west Texas. My brother Jerry (from southeast Texas) met us there and shared a room with me. We both snore, but otherwise it worked out well. All my siblings and most of our kids are sci-fi fans, and Jerry, a professional writer, has written some sci-fi. We had a wonderful time, and Jerry sold some of his books. I got copies of his books for free, one perk of being his little sister.

The convention center was populated with strange, wonderful people, many of them in odd and colorful costumes. Our cousins were even more wonderful. We met the two cousins with whom I had been in touch, Swede Carlson and Charles Carlson, and a bonus third cousin, Charles Boettcher. They were dressed like ordinary people, which was a relief after seeing some of the convention attendees.

We were very happy that they were able to meet with us on fairly short notice. We felt instantly comfortable with all these newly discovered Swedish-American relatives, and they made lasting impressions on us. We heard some great family stories. We particularly enjoyed learning how many things we had in common.

Charles Carlson and his wife Kathy met us for lunch in San Antonio while we were at the convention. Charles is the son of my grandfather's brother Richard. He is about my age, but technically belongs to an earlier generation. Richard and his wife had Charles at a time when Richard's siblings were having grandchildren.

After the convention Jerry went to a writer's meeting some-place else in Texas. Sue, Beth and I drove to Elgin, Texas, and met Swede Carlson, his wife Sally and daughter Jenny, as well as Charles Boettcher and his wife Beth. Swede and Charles B. are grandsons of my grandfather's brother Arvid. Beth is the family historian and has saved a lot of documents and notes, so she was able to share some Carlson family history with us.

Part of downtown Elgin

The cousins drove us through the town of Elgin to see places of historic interest and eat some great barbecue. The next day Swede and Sally took us all over the surrounding area, which was settled by Swedes in the mid to late 1800s. We walked around the Lund farm once owned by our great grandfather Carl August Carlson (on Carlson Road), and met the current owners, also Swedish/Americans. We went by the old Johnson farm, once belonging to Swede's maternal grandparents (also Swedes), and now owned by Swede and Sally. We said hello to Swede's cattle when they gathered round his truck to share some bags of feed. We admired the mustang grapes growing by the road. We visited several historic churches, and saw some old schools and farmhouses. We walked through two Swedish/American cemeteries, and noticed several more as we drove along. Those cemeteries are the only places I have ever seen the Swedish flag flying.

Swedes in central Texas mostly grew cotton, but other crops did well too: sorghum, vegetables, broomcorn, stone fruits, nuts, corn and wheat. The farm country we saw around Elgin was beautiful. It was also very hot in August. If it had not been for air conditioning in our vehicles, none of us would have survived the day!

Swede told us that Elgin is pronounced with a hard G. He

warned us that if we mispronounced it, locals would think we were ignorant and un-cool.

The Lund Lutheran Church

As we walked in the Lund church cemetery Swede found a small rattlesnake among the graves, and warned all of us to watch where we stepped. The event reminded me that early Texas farmers lived in a time with no anti-venin available should they be bitten. They also lacked mosquito repellent, fly spray, sunscreen, tornado warning systems, and indoor toilets. The families had their share of tragedy, including premature deaths, illnesses, crop losses, and financial problems. But our Swedish progenitors flourished in Texas despite such difficulties. They played an important role in the state's development from a frontier state to one of the world's largest economies. I am proud to be descended from such tenacious and industrious folk.

The cemetery across from the Lund Lutheran Church

Several months after that visit, I located two more cousins. One was Peggy McManus, the granddaughter of Verner Carlson, Oscar's oldest brother. The other was another Charles Carlson from Oregon. He is a cousin through my grandmother's Engblom family, completely unrelated to the Carlsons of Oscar's family, and not to be confused with the Charles Carlson I met in San Antonio.

Chuck and his wife Edith are both chemists. They stopped at my house in August of 2014, while on their way to an American Chemical Society meeting. They are retired, but still keep up with the latest research and see old friends and colleagues when possible. They are both genealogy nuts, and Chuck was helpful in correcting my mistakes about the Westling children.

Fortunately the chemist Charles Carlson prefers to be called Chuck, which lessens my confusion. His great grandmother and my great grandmother were sisters, and his mother remembered playing with my mother in Lund at the family farm. Our great grandmothers were daughters of John (Jonas) Westling, who settled in Lund in 1889, eight years before my great grandfather Carl August Carlson bought his farm there. The Westlings, Engbloms and Carlsons all knew each other and attended the same Lutheran church. The families were related through marriage. How wonderful that after one hundred twenty-five years their descendants are finding each other!

## Researching Swedish Texans

One recurrent problem is that some Swedish names are very common. There are a lot of Carlsons and Engbloms, and many Swedes named their children Carl, Charles and Charlotte. These particular three names are all forms of the same Old Norse name, Karl, meaning "free man." Distinguishing my relatives from other Swedish/Americans was sometimes tricky.

Another issue is that I don't read Swedish, so old Swedish church records (those that have been digitized and made available online) are not comprehensible. I was unable to trace any farther back than my great-great grandfather on the Carlson side. If my cousin Charles (from the Carlson side, not the Engblom one) makes his planned trip to Sweden, he might be able to find ancestral names going back farther in time. Swedish churches have maintained careful records of births, marriages and deaths.

I have not tried to make this a truly scholarly work by referencing every fact or date, because that makes for cumbersome reading and I am a lazy writer. Instead, I listed the sources I used at the end of this document. But some of my sources are worth mentioning here. If you are interested in more details of Swedish/Texan history, these are some excellent websites and books to consider.

One especially useful source was a book titled *Svenskarne i Texas i ord och bild, 1838-1918*. In English, this is *Swedes in Texas in Words and Pictures*. It was published in 1918, in Swedish, and was recently translated into English and made available online.

The book includes a lot of general history about Swedish Texans, the communities they founded, and hundreds of short biographies, including some of my relatives. These are not unbiased views. The biographies are all complimentary, and everyone is described as hard working and pleasant. Particular note was made of a person's regular attendance at church. Apparently nobody included in the book was a felon, a ne'er-do-well, or even rude.

The editor (John Melcham Öjerholm) and his team of interviewers and writers worked for three years and interviewed hundreds of people to produce this 1200 page book. They included photographs of Swedish Texans and in some cases, their homes and businesses. Later sociological researchers have criticized Öjerholm's book for ignoring so many Swedish single men, widowers and widows, and farm hands. In spite of this shortcoming, the book is a fascinating look at Texas Swedes in the late 19th and early 20th centuries. Nothing terribly scandalous was written, but there was a heavy dose of sentimentality, in the style of newspapers and books of the time.

My grandfather had a red-bound copy of the book but after

he died, there was nobody in my immediate family who could read Swedish. Sue thinks the book was given to one of Richard's sons. I remember looking at the book as a child, and seeing photographs of family members I had never met. All of them looked very serious and dignified, in the fashion of early 1900s formal photographs.

Öjerholm was a Methodist minister who immigrated to America in 1883. He served many years as the editor of the *Posten*, a Swedish language newspaper published in Austin. He spent his life promoting the retention of Swedish culture in central Texas.

The book starts with a detailed Texas history, in which Native Americans are dismissed as inferior beings that "lacked all culture necessary for history." Öjerholm included a description of Texas geography, agriculture and industry, state government, the education system, and a history of all the Texas Swedish churches. Reading the material will give you a taste of the general attitudes of the time.

In June of 1917, an energetic group of Swedish/Americans, including Öjerholm, organized the first Swedish Pioneers Reunion in Round Rock, Texas, to celebrate the fiftieth year since the first Swedes arrived. The event was a big success, and a similar reunion has been held every year since then. In 1937, the one hundredth anniversary of S.M. Swenson's arrival in Texas, the reunion organizers formed an official non-profit organization called the Texas Swedish Pioneers Association. Swenson was instrumental in bringing the first Swedes to Texas.

The Association, headquartered in Austin, manages the

annual summer reunion. It maintains a website:

www.swedesintexas.com

This includes articles on why Swedish Texans emigrated, the dangers and difficulties they faced, and some first hand accounts. The website has the entire *Swedes in Texas* book (translated into English) and digital versions of all the original photographs.

Early Swedish Pioneers Reunions began with a Lutheran church service in Swedish and included a "varukorg middag" (basket dinner) and speeches by local Swedish/American leaders in education and politics. Sometimes non-Swedish politicians showed up, hoping to garner some votes. Now these reunions are in English (except for the singing) but the Association tries to include some aspects of Swedish culture in each one. Food is always involved, as in most meetings involving Swedes.

When we toured Elgin with Swede and Sally, we visited the Elgin Historical Museum. I purchased several small books published by the Elgin Historical Society, including *A History of Elgin, Texas, 1872-1972*. This is an interesting look at how a small town grew quickly out of empty prairie and became an important hub for sending cotton and other crops off to market. The town is still small, but growing as a bedroom community for people employed in the greater Austin area. Sadly, much of the farmland is being converted to housing developments.

The Elgin museum folks (mainly volunteers) were very helpful to us. Swede was especially happy to locate high school yearbook photos of his father, Roland Carlson (also called "Big Swede," or "Broom" because he and his father Arvid grew broomcorn).

The Texas State Historical Association supports a site called "Digital Gateway to Texas History." This site is easy to use, well organized, and nicely written. It has several documents devoted to Swedish immigrants to Texas.

An invaluable source was the *Swedish American Historical Quarterly*, published by a Chicago nonprofit, the Swedish American Historical Society. This scholarly journal has been in print since 1950. Texts of the articles up to 2003 are available online for free.

*The Swedish Texans,* by Larry Scott (published in 1990) is a publication of the University of Texas Institute of Texas Cultures. I found information about the Westling family in this book, and also a clear description of each of the small Texas towns built by Swedes. The book includes quotes from the early Swedish settlers, describing the land, their farms, struggles, and successes. I cannot recommend this book enough, to anyone with an interest in the subject.

The cousins I mentioned earlier have been generous in sharing documents, photographs, and stories. Peggy McManus kindly sent me a copy of a letter Mama sent to her in the 1990s, as well as all the information she had accumulated. Peggy has been researching the Carlsons since before the Internet made such work simpler.

Mama wrote down some of her family stories in the 1990s when she took a community college class called "Writing Your Memories." My sister Sue taught the class, and she convinced Mama to take it. It was designed for seniors, and was part of Howard College's effort to preserve Texas history. Mama made Sue promise not to tell the other students in the class that they were related. She was afraid they would think Mama was getting special treatment. Considering that nobody in the class (except Sue) was a day under seventy, and there was no actual grade given, this was an unnecessary precaution. Sue made sure that all of Mama's children got a copy of her class essays.

I kept the letters Mama sent me after I moved to California in the 1970s. Most of them were just current news about which great grandchild said something entertaining, relatives' health problems, scandal about the neighbors, or the latest tornado, hail or dust storm in Big Spring. But some of the letters are reiterations of old family stories.

In her letters and essays, Mama gave details about places, years and events, many of which I found to be accurate when I looked at official records. Sometimes she got a year wrong, or misspelled a name, and she frequently added some drama to make the stories "better." She had a habit of telling her children and grandchildren really gory and terrible stories. My brother Jerry says that all of Mama's stories seemed to have blood gushing, a tragic death, or both.

I have tried to make clear which parts of her stories I find incredible. Some of them I have not included at all. I have been so skeptical of her tales that when I find details that are accurate, I am somewhat surprised!

Where I could locate them, I wanted to include signatures. For the Carlson men, these were from WW I draft registration cards. I find their old fashioned handwriting interesting, and believe that cursive writing will be a lost art within the next few decades, since now people type everything.

## Some Swedish History

Europe has been periodically covered in ice, and the last glacial period ended about 10,000 years ago. Scandinavia, which includes Norway, Sweden, Finland, and part of Russia, thawed out last. Starting about 9,000 years ago plant life had become well enough established that animals and people could survive. During the Stone Age, groups of hunter-gatherers from south of the Baltic Sea moved into Scandinavia. Genetic studies show that people in southern Sweden are closely related to those in Germany, Norway, Denmark, Netherlands and England. The northern Scandinavian/ Russian Sami people (also called Laplanders) are a distinctive genetic group closely related to the Finns.

Archaeologists have found evidence of several distinct groups of Stone Age hunter/gatherers in Sweden, and by 500 BC there were fairly advanced societies making metal tools, pottery, boats, and interesting petro glyphs. We know that even the very early Scandia people were great traders and traveled considerable distances, because they carried Baltic amber as far away as the Mediterranean.

Swedish, German, Norwegian, Icelandic and Danish are all linguistic descendants of Old Norse, a language spoken by Scandinavians during the Viking Era between about 800 and 1000 AD.

By the 1300s, Old Norse began differentiating into various daughter tongues, and at the same time strongly influenced English, Scottish Gaelic and French. The Norsemen (North men) settled in Scandinavia and moved outward into what are now Great Britain, mainland Europe, and Greenland. "Normandy," which is now France, was named for the Norsemen.

Finns and Swedes have intermarried a lot, but the two groups have different genetic and linguistic origins. The Finns speak a Uralic language related to Hungarian and Estonian and originating some-where in the Ural Mountains, which run from the Arctic Ocean through Russia and form the traditional boundary between Europe and Asia.

The distress my Swedish ancestors had when a half Finnish man married into their family had its roots in the time (from Middle Ages till early 1800s) when Sweden ruled Finland. There is still a traditional rivalry between Sweden and Finland, but it is seen today mainly during soccer games. It is a taken about as seriously as the competition between Texas Aggies and the Arkansas Razorbacks.

The fearsome Vikings who plundered Britain in the 8th century were from what is today Denmark, Sweden and Norway. Most of them were pagans. By the end of Viking times, Sweden was an established country with a Christian king.

In the early 1700s a Swedish king installed the Lutheran Church as the official church of Sweden, and pretty much kicked out the Catholics. Many of the Swedes who came to the United States in the 1800s (including the Carlsons) were Lutherans. The history of the Lutheran Church is fascinating and worth some study, but I cannot include it here.

Sweden's borders have expanded and contracted over time. During the 1600s it included parts of Germany, Poland, Russia and Finland. Modern borders were established in 1809, when Sweden and Finland separated.

Sweden's last participation in a European battlefield (except for soldiers in United Nations Peacekeeping forces) was in the early 1800s during the Napoleonic wars. Europe was an untidy mess for over a decade and thousands of people were killed from war, hunger and disease. Sweden was allied with the U. K., Austria, Prussia, Spain, and Russia against Napoleon. Since that time Sweden has maintained a strict policy of nonaggression and neutrality, even through both World Wars.

The monarchy became a constitutional one in the nineteenth century, responding to pressure from its citizens. Modern Sweden is known for its progressive social policies, cleanliness and ethnic tolerance. It has some of the last remaining true wilderness areas in Europe. Sweden is way ahead of most other nations in environmental protection, but suffers from acidified rain and snow caused by air pollution blown up from southern Europe.

The medieval class system in Sweden was different from the rest of Europe; the peasants were not serfs. European serfs formed the lowest rung of society, with few rights and no hope of moving up socially and economically. Serfs were essentially owned by the nobility in a form of slavery that persisted in Eastern Europe until the 1800s. In contrast, Sweden's peasants always had the possibility of making better lives for themselves. This difference in social history helps explain the uppity attitude of Swedes in general, and their skeptical view of authority and upper class conceit.

Sweden's medieval Crown owned all the nation's land, and peasants rented their farms. As you might expect, some people were more effective farmers than others, and so they made more money. If a medieval peasant got wealthy enough, he could buy a title, and he could bequeath that exalted position to his offspring. As in other European nations, a heroic soldier or a king's favorite might also be rewarded with a title. But Sweden has always limited its nobility, so there have never been very many barons or dukes. The noble class was called "frälse," meaning "freeneck." (Frälse is pronounced "frell-sa," with a slightly rolled "r.")

In modern times, having an inherited title may give a Swede a bit more cachet in some circles, but there are no innate advantages. However, until 2003, there were some legal privileges that frälse enjoyed, including the right to be executed by beheading rather than hanging. This gives a whole new meaning to "free-neck."

During the early 1600s, the Swedish king began giving large tracts of land to the frälse as rewards for financial and military support. Nobility were exempt from land taxes, and peasants were still not allowed to own land. This was not a very smart plan, since the resulting tax income was reduced. The system was doomed to eventual failure.

King Charles (or Carl) XI ruled the Swedish Empire in the late 1600s. Charles XI was actually only the fifth Swedish king named Charles, because his great grandfather made up a number so his line looked more ancient and respectable. Nobody in later generations corrected him. The current king is named Carl XVI, but is more accurately named Carl XI.

Charles XI inherited a chaotic muddle. His father died young and Charles was forced to grow up quickly. He managed, despite an inauspicious beginning, to make some major changes in the way Sweden's finances and foreign policy were run.

King Charles XI

Charles XI took back much of the former Crown land from his nobles with a series of laws called the Reductions. The frälse were not happy about losing their lucrative properties, but Charles needed a way to bail out the Swedish economy, which had been wrecked from years of warfare. Some of the land he confiscated went to soldiers as payment for military service. This was a huge incentive for peasants to take military service and it freed the treasury from having to pay them in cash. The new landowners were called freeholders; they owned the land, but were not royal or noble.

It may seem surprising that there was no rebellion against the Reductions, when so many nobles were financially ruined. However, the move was strongly supported by everyone who was not frälse, including peasants, tradesmen, and upper level state employees, and the actual numbers of frälse were small. The great aristocratic families were viewed as having too much power over other Swedes, and the lower class folks had little sympathy for their plight.

Besides giving land to soldiers, the Crown began selling farms to the peasant tenant farmers who had previously been working that land. Farmers got a fair deal on the cost. This provided an incentive to buy land, and in the long term, the Crown was better off. The land was constantly productive and tax income more predictable. The long-standing tax exemption for free necks was rescinded.

By 1700, a third of Swedish land belonged to freeholders, and by 1815, they owned three quarters of Swedish arable land. This helped peasants to have somewhat better lives, but Sweden remained a relatively poor nation due to its northern latitude and cold climate. Farming was (and still is) more productive in Europe's southern countries. Even the most southern part of Sweden has a relatively short growing season, and the soil is thin and rocky. Northern Sweden is colder and even worse for crops, although coniferous forests thrive.

In the late 1600s Countess Eva Ekeblad, a scientist and the first female member of the Royal Swedish Academy of Sciences, invented a way to make both flour and alcohol from Andean potatoes. Historians disagree on the exact origins of vodka, but surely the Countess deserves some credit. Eva helped introduce the potato as a food staple in Sweden. Potatoes grow well in poor rocky soil and cool climates.

The Countess

Until the potato was introduced, the poor people of Sweden made "bark bread." This was a flatbread made from whatever grain was available, plus the ground up inner bark from trees and sometimes some dried lichen. The inner bark had some phloem tissue, which is what carries sugars through a tree, and so there was some small nutritive value. But it was mainly fiber and served as a belly-filler. Between 1750 and 1850, the entire population of Europe increased because of the potato, and bark bread was almost unheard of. Sweden's population doubled.

Swedish children eating bark bread, late 1800s

Ireland's population boom was followed by a major famine in the 1840s when all the Irish potato crops were killed by blight. Sweden was spared the potato blight, but hunger and starvation arrived by the 1860s anyway when the population exceeded the capacity of Swedish soil to feed everyone.

Adding to the population growth was the advent of smallpox vaccinations, so more people survived childhood. Also, by the early 1800s no more Swedish men were being sent off to die in war. Instead, they stayed home, married, grew potatoes and produced more Swedes.

Sweden in the mid 1800s was poor, crowded and hungry, as was most of Europe. Once the United States passed the Homestead Act in 1862, fifty million Europeans immigrated. The Act allowed anyone to file for ownership of 160 acres of free American land, if he could occupy it, dig a well, plow 10 acres, and live there for five years. Most of the Swedes coming to the United States settled in the Midwest, forming a number of "Svenskamerika" communities. The Swedes who came to Texas were, of course, the cream of the crop. Immigration was encouraged by Americans wanting to hire laborers or sell farmland, and advertisements like the one below were printed all over Europe.

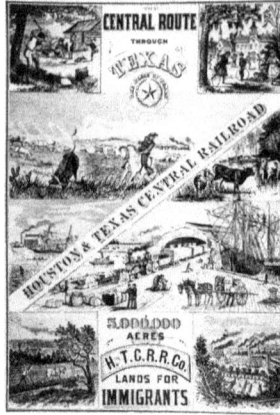

There were three peaks of immigration to America from Sweden. The first occurred in the late 1860s, a second one during the Long Depression in the late 1880s, and the last in the early 1900s.

The first peak was due to a trio of seriously bad years in Europe. 1867 was a year of heavy rains that rotted crops in the fields. In 1868 there was severe drought, and crops died again. 1869 was a year of epidemics, which always follow hunger. Cholera, diphtheria, smallpox (because mandatory vaccinations were not enforced), scarlet fever, typhoid fever, tuberculosis, and other diseases killed people already weakened by starvation.

The second peak of immigration occurred after a worldwide depression created a crisis in the steel, forest and sawmill industries in Sweden. Bankruptcies in the sawmill business were common. The Carlsons emigrated during this second period, after Carl August lost most of his money in some business speculations.

The third peak, in the early 1900s, was stimulated by a recession. Workers in forestry, textile and metal industries had their wages slashed. In 1909 there were a series of labor strikes over a three-month period.

My great grandparents Carl August and Matilda married in 1873, only five years after the trio of terrible years. They had their first child a year later, and another baby came along every two or three years after that. In 1888, after producing six children, the family left Sweden. Carl August Carlson was a well educated, intelligent, hard-working man, and he worked in a variety of jobs besides farming. Every one of his children was expected to work for the common good of the family. But Carl and Matilda must have worried about what the future would hold for their kids. It was a very tough time for most Swedes.

Over a million Swedes emigrated during the late 19th and early 20th centuries. Before 1830, it was actually illegal for Swedish families to emigrate. But the government, fearing a Malthusian catastrophe, wisely rescinded the anti-emigration law.

Between 1840 and 1940, one out of every five Swedes left their homeland. A relatively small number settled in Texas, but now over 160,000 people in Texas claim Swedish ancestry. Swedish-American farmers had big families, and with the better farmland in America, more of their children survived. The Swedes remaining in Sweden had less competition for farmland, food and space, so they benefitted also.

For Swedes coming to America, the primary lure was inexpensive, fertile land. Swedish arable acreage was limited, and families who owned land could not divide it into large enough bits so each adult child could make a living.

But there were other reasons for emigration. One was a desire to leave the Crown's authoritarian monarchy and live in a more democratic nation. Religious freedom was another spur. The state Lutheran church was so repressive that for decades it was actually illegal for a person to leave it! The laws loosened a bit in 1860, so people were allowed to leave the church, but only if they joined another officially recognized church. The temperance movement in Sweden, which discouraged alcohol, may have played a part as well. Sweden and Norway were the first European nations to have temperance organizations. Starting in 1855, it was illegal to make home brewed alcoholic beverages.

Swedish peasants were much better educated than people in other parts of Europe. Starting in 1842, eight years of elementary school public education for boys and girls was compulsory. Most of that education was through church schools. Swedes read newspapers and books, and kept up on what was happening elsewhere in the world. They wanted a better deal.

Swedish immigration to America formed a chain: one immigrant family would write home and tell their relatives, who then came and encouraged other relatives and friends to make the journey. Many immigrants sent money to other family members in Sweden for the cost of passage. American companies actively advertised in Sweden, looking for lumberjacks, miners, farmers, railroad workers and skilled craftsmen, and sometimes offered to pay their passage.

Transportation to America in the mid 1800s was much easier than it had been for previous generations of European immigrants. Several major steamship lines were in business by the end of the 1860s, and each huge ocean liner one could carry hundreds of people, thus dropping the price per ticket enough that even relatively poor people could afford the trip. It took two or three weeks on a steam ship to reach America, compared to three months on a sailing ship.

Steamship circa 1880

Immigration to the U. S. became a kind of craze during the late 1800s in Sweden. It was called "American Fever." Wealthier industrialists and landowners disapproved of it, because their cheap labor pool was depleted. In some frälse families, children who emigrated were disinherited and lost their titles. There were numerous articles and books published telling how miserable immigrant Swedes were in America. These did nothing to stem the outflow.

In 1907, Sweden established a Parliamentary Commission to investigate how to prevent Swedes from leaving. As a result, some changes occurred: better housing, voting rights for the poor (still males only at that time), and broader education. These things, plus the beginning of World War I, slowed the leakage of Swedes to America.

Starting just before WW II, the trend actually reversed. People from many other countries began moving to Sweden. They had varying motives; some were escaping war and possible death, others seeking a place with better employment opportunities. The first wave of new immigrants came from the Baltic countries invaded by Germany. Shortly after, thousands of Danish Jews and Finnish children were evacuated to Sweden. Many of those fleeing the war in Europe remained in Sweden after the war was over.

After WW II when the Soviet Union invaded Hungary and Czechoslovakia, political refugees from those countries found safe haven in Sweden. During the Viet Nam war, there were American draft dodgers, and in 1972 Chileans came, escaping the violent political coup against President Allende. In more recent years, immigrants have come from Yugoslavia, Iraq, Iran, Syria, Bosnia, Somalia, Turkey, Serbia, and Albania. Since about 2004, the city of Södertälje (with about 80,000 people) has taken in more Iraqi refugees than the United States and Canada combined.

The exact numbers are hard to know because Sweden does not keep records of ethnicities in its censuses. But an unofficial survey made in 2011 showed that about 20% of Swedes were of at least partly foreign descent. Some of the larger cities have had major cultural changes as a result of immigration, and the previously homogenous white Lutheran population has become much more varied.

Sweden has a liberal social welfare program, and the state has tried to help integrate new immigrants. But the foreign-born are usually poor. They often arrive with little education, no job skills, and no Swedish. They tend to congregate in larger cities, in neighborhoods composed of their own ethnicities. The government has built housing projects that have turned into immigrant ghettos. Anti-immigrant feelings and hate crimes have increased. In 2013, there were several riots, instigated by unemployed, frustrated youthful immigrants. It will be interesting to see how the state handles these inevitable assimilation problems, many of which have been (and still are) faced in the United States.

## The Texas Swedes

Swedes found central Texas weather very odd. Summers were hot and humid and winters were short and mild, a complete change from the climate in Sweden. The new immigrants experienced droughts, hailstones so large they could kill a cow, tornados, torrential rains that made boot-sucking mud, and strong wind. One immigrant wrote home that sometimes in Texas the wind blew so hard he could not open his front door.

Balanced against these extremes were the thousands of acres of empty land, rivers, rich soil, trees, fish, edible wild animals, and abundant natural beauty.

The size of the Swedish community in central Texas was largely due to a couple of famous and influential Swedes: Swen Magnus Swenson and his uncle Swante Palm, who was about the same age. (Swante, Svante, Swen and Sven are all based on a common Nordic name meaning "young warrior.") These two men were incredibly important in Swedish-American and Texas history. They were the reason Texas has more citizens of Swedish descent than any other southern state. All Swedish Texans should know a bit about them.

Swen Swenson (left) and his uncle Swante Palm

Swenson's life was a classic "poor immigrant makes good" story. He arrived penniless in New York in the mid 1830s. He learned English and worked for a while as a bookkeeper and mercantile clerk. Then he moved to the Texas frontier and married a wealthy widow with a cotton plantation. In the 1840s he cleverly bought thousands of cheap acres in the newly independent republic of Texas. Texas became a state in 1845, and the 1850s were a decade of relative prosperity and growth. By 1860, Swenson owned almost 230,000 acres of land around Austin, and 500,000 acres in west Texas. Swenson founded the well-known and enormous SMS ranches in west Texas. He planted pecan orchards and shipped native Texas pecans to other states, establishing that nut as a nationally desirable food item and no doubt spreading the popularity of pecan pies, one of the eminent gastronomic treasures of the American south.

Swenson owned slaves, but did not like the institution of slavery. This was not just a humanitarian attitude; he found that slaves did not work as hard as free men. The idea of hiring fellow Swedes to work in his cotton fields was attractive, and his friend Sam Houston encouraged the idea of recruiting Swedish farmers to settle in central Texas. Houston figured that other Swedes would be as hardworking as Swenson. Swenson knew exactly how terrible were the conditions in his home province of Småland, and assumed that many of his relatives and their neighbors would welcome a new start. Beginning in 1848, Swenson loaned the passage costs to hundreds of Swedes. Many were single young men and women, but entire families immigrated. They paid him back by working a year on the land he owned, and most of them bought land from him eventually. In essence, the first Swedes were brought to Texas as substitutes for black slaves, although there were undoubtedly more complex reasons in Swenson's head.

The Civil War (1861-65) temporarily slowed Swedish immigration to Texas. Swenson actually moved to Mexico during the war because his anti-slavery views were so unpopular and he had received credible death threats from Confederate sympathizers. Before he left, he buried a huge amount of gold under his fireplace. His uncle Swante Palm later dug it up and sent it to him. The exact amount of gold is not well documented, but seems to have increased as the story was told over and over.

Starting in 1867, Swante Palm and another of Swenson's uncles in Sweden ran an immigration service that has been termed the "Swedish Pipeline." Most of the Swedes they brought across the Atlantic were from their own home province of Småland, in southern Sweden, where the economic situation was particularly bad.

Swante Palm, an almost pathological bibliophile, is well remembered for having left his enormous library (10,000 books) to the University of Texas. It more than doubled the size of the new University's collection. He changed his last name to Palm when he came to America, and his later-arriving relatives took the name also.

Swenson's and Palm's countrymen and women settled in central Texas near Austin (where Swenson owned an astonishing amount of land) and helped establish several rural communities. North of Austin, in Williamson County, settlements were built along Brushy Creek, and included communities like Hutto, Jonah, Taylor, Round Rock, Palm Valley, and Govalle. East of Austin, in Travis

County, the settlements of Lund, Elgin, and New Sweden were formed somewhat later.

In the early 1850s, Anna Palm and her six sons settled close to Brushy Creek, north of Austin, and other Swedes followed. Anna's husband Anders, who tragically died of cholera soon after she and her children came to Texas, was one of Swante Palm's brothers. The community became known as Palm Valley. The Palms helped establish the Palm Valley Lutheran Church and a small town called Palm Valley, which is now a ghost town. Palm Valley is about a mile west of Round Rock, which is also on the creek. Anna Palm is renowned as a tough pioneer woman.

The city of Round Rock is named for a large boulder in Brushy Creek, marking a shallow area for crossing with wagons, horse and cattle. After the Civil War, the Round Rock crossing became part of the famous Chisholm Trail, a route used for moving Texas cattle to Abilene, Kansas. Round Rock is now a bedroom community for Austin.

The famous round rock in Brushy Creek

Old records sometimes used Brushy Creek, Georgetown, and Round Rock interchangeably, for people living on farms nearby. The Lund church registry for the Carlsons says the family moved from Brushy Creek, but the 1918 book *Swedes in Texas* says they came from Round Rock. The name Brushy Creek is now a census-designation for about 9 square miles of farmland, all bordering the creek.

Palm Valley Lutheran Church, founded by the early Swedes coming to the Brushy Creek area, is a beautiful red brick building with an imposing steeple and immaculate grounds. My sister Sue, her daughter Beth and I visited the church in 2012, along with cousins Charles B., Swede, and their wives. The cemetery is filled with Swedes, including a number of our relatives.

Elroy Heveriah, a retired pastor from the Palm Valley church, recently wrote a book called *Anna's Journey*. It is a well-researched, historically accurate description of Anna Palm's move to Texas with her family in 1848. Heveriah's book helped me understand the hardships the early Swedes experienced, although my people came forty years later than did the Palms and had an easier time. We saw Anna's grave at the Palm Valley church.

Palm Valley
Lutheran Church

The tiny community of Lund, Texas, is where the Westlings, Carlsons and Engbloms lived and farmed. It is only a few miles from

Elgin. The countryside around Lund in the 1880s was described in *Swedes in Texas*:

"The bushes were so thick and the land was so full of cactus that they had to clear it with an axe to make way. In this wilderness, where rattlesnakes were abundant, there is now a group of wealthy and satisfied Swedish-American people living in nice and modern homes. The rattlesnakes and the cactus have had to make room for the beautiful and green cotton plant which grows, blooms and makes the well-kept farms a sea of white."

Swedes coming to Texas in the 1840s traveled by ship from Sweden to Liverpool, England, then on to New York. They took another ship down the American coast, around Florida, and landed in Galveston. Then they took smaller boats up Buffalo Bayou to Houston and finally travelled overland in wagons to central Texas. It was a long and difficult journey. On the way, they risked shipwreck, poor food, cholera, thirst, malaria, yellow fever, bandits, boredom, drunken sailors, rattlesnakes, lost belongings, homesickness, culture shock, and Texas weather.

Sailing ships crossing the Atlantic were eventually replaced by steamships, which were faster and more comfortable for passengers. The grueling boat and wagon ride across Texas was eliminated when railroads were built. By the time my Carlson ancestors arrived in the late 1880s, Texas had a good railroad system from the coast to the state capital. The railroad network was incredibly important in stimulating Texan economic growth. Swante Swenson invested in early Texas railroads and made a bundle.

As Sam Houston had predicted, Swedes made excellent Texans. They were hard working, literate, religious, valued education, arts and music, and paid their taxes. Many were fine craftsmen, and helped in the construction of homes, businesses and public buildings. Swedes tended to be involved in their communities. Swedes have been generally good at saving important documents, which has been useful to genealogists.

The website Nordic.com tells the story of a young Swedish-speaking black man, Will Palm (raised by Sven William Palm of Round Rock) who was sent down to meet newly arrived Swedes at the Austin railway station. This was just after the Civil War. Will spoke in perfect "Småländska Swedish" and told the newcomers (most of whom had never seen a black person) that, "after a few Texas summers, you will be as black as I am!"

Mama told the same story about her grandmother Lotten, just getting off the ship on the east coast and meeting a black man for the first time. Mama must have remembered hearing the story when she was a child, and adapted it to her own family.

Swedes in central Texas held on to their language and customs for a relatively long time, compared to immigrants from other countries. For three generations, Texas Swedes could read a Swedish language newspaper (the *Posten*) published in Austin, and visit bakeries and shoe repair shops with Swedish-speaking clerks. Many banks, stores and grocery stores had Swedish-speaking employees. In 1900, Swedish businesses were common in central Texas. Lutheran churches had Swedish services. But by the 1920s, Texas Swedes had begun to integrate. They married non-Swedes, their children spoke English, and their church services were almost universally held in English.

## Our Carlsons

Like most other Swedes, Carl August and Matilda's children and grandchildren were smart, generous, unpretentious and joyful people. They loved music and enjoyed gardening, strong coffee and good food. They had a powerful work ethic and tended to be politically conservative and religious. Most were animal lovers, and kept pet dogs or cats. Without exception, they loved story telling and a good joke. The tradition of Texas Tall Tales is one that Texas Swedes embraced. I suspect that the Swedes may have invented it first.

Scandinavians tend to be taller than other Europeans. The Carlson kids were all tall people, with square jaws, fair skin, and light brown, red or blonde hair. They burned easily in the Texas sun. Carlsons tended toward large bones, big hands, and were physically strong. My grandfather, who was 5 feet 11 inches, was considered undersized.

Several of the Carlsons had crooked teeth and an overbite. My mother had braces on her baby teeth. All her children and some of her grandchildren and great grandchildren had irregular teeth.

The children and grandchildren of my grandfather's generation are a hybrid blend. Swedish genes are mingled with those from other Europeans, Africans, Asians and Native Americans. I cannot blame all the orthodontic bills on Carlson genes. Still, I can see physical resemblances between the male Carlson cousins I have met and my own brothers. They all have the same broad, sturdy hands.

Carl August and his wife Matilda did not live particularly long lives; she died at 53 and he died at 67. But their children exceeded average life expectancy for people of their times, in spite of having a genetic tendency toward high cholesterol, atherosclerosis (fatty deposits in the arteries) and arteriosclerosis (arterial hardening and loss of flexibility), which can lead to death by heart attack or stroke. Cardiovascular disease killed Matilda, four of her children, and several of her grandchildren.

All four of Mama's children take cholesterol-lowering medication. We are hoping to postpone the illnesses that inevitably result from plaque, such as stroke, heart attack, and kidney disease. Of course, diet plays a role also. We all remember our grandfather Oscar's high fat diet and his favorite snack, toasted bread spread with bacon fat.

Another significant family trait is the tendency toward addiction. My grandfather and my mother were both addicted to tobacco, and were life long smokers. Three of Carl August's sons (Oscar, Arvid and Richard) were alcoholics, and the genes for addiction were passed on to a number of their descendants in the following generations. The three brothers were functional alcoholics, so were able to work and maintain a reasonably normal place in society, but their families suffered. I am amazed that in spite of years of abusing alcohol, the inebriate Carlson brothers lived so long.

## The Carlsons' Birthplaces

My great grandfather Carl August Carlson was born in the province of Östergötland, in the härad (region) of Göstrings, and near the village (or parish) of Ekebyborna.

Östergötland is a largely agricultural province in southern Sweden. It is pronounced "ostee yot lund." The northern part of the province is hilly and forested, and the south is dotted with hundreds of lakes and streams. The province is famous for its fishing. I assume the Carlsons were fishermen before coming to Texas. Certainly some of them continued their enthusiasm for fishing after they emigrated.

Östergötland farmhouse and stream

Since medieval times, Östergötland has been Scandinavia's breadbox. A wide strip of plain in the middle of Östergötland, running east to west, has long been used for growing rye, oats, wheat, barley and potatoes. Östergötlanders are supposed to make the world's best potato pancakes. In recent years, bio-fuel crops have begun to occupy more acreage.

The name Östergötland has an interesting origin. It can be translated as "eastern land of the Götar." The term Götar means something like "men with lots of semen." The Götars were a Germanic ethnic group dating from late Viking times.

Östergötland has the enormous Lake Vättern on its western edge, and its east coast is the Gulf of Bothnia, a part of the Baltic Sea. Lake Vättern is the second largest lake in Sweden.

Östergötland province, with Lake Vättern to the west

Farm on the edge of Lake Vättern

The word härad (meaning "one hundred") is German in origin and was used, with varying pronunciations and spellings, all over Europe in the past. It originally referred to the land required to support a hundred families, and was a unit intermediate in size between a parish and a county. There were once about two-dozen härads in the province of Östergötland.

Ekebyborna, Carl August's birthplace, is one of several tiny rural parishes in the härad of Göstrings, on the south shore of Lake Boren, a smaller lake on the northeast side of Lake Vättern. The area today includes pastures and agricultural fields, as well as nature preserves. It is a great place for birders.

Ekebyborna Lutheran Church

Ekebyborna is relatively well known because the famous medieval visionary Saint Birgitta (Bridget) lived there. In her visions of the Virgin Mary, she saw the mother of Christ as a fair-skinned, blonde, Swedish-looking woman, and her colorful description strongly influenced the western image of the nativity. Both Catholics and Lutherans honor Saint Birgitta.

Saint Birgitta

Carl August's wife Matilda was born in the beautiful parish of Åsbo, about 30 miles from Ekebyborna. At the time of her birth the region was well known for woodworking and the production of casks, furniture, and, oddly enough, rakes.

Åsbo church and countryside.

The Göta Canal, built in the early 1800s, crosses Östergötland. The canal forms a continuous pathway through rivers and lakes from the west coast to the east coast of Sweden, and includes Lake Boren. The canal and lake system is called "sveriges blå band," meaning "Sweden's Blue Ribbon." Building the canal was a stupendous effort, and required twenty-two years to complete. It was finished in 1832, only a few years before the railways were built. My mother told me about her Engblom grandmother (Lotten) travelling on the canal with her father when he was working as a trader. Railways eventually replaced the canal as a way of moving most produce and manufactured goods, but the canal is still used and is a popular tourist attraction.

Two sections of the Göta Canal

Sweden was later than the rest of Europe to develop a railway system. In fact, the railways there were being built at about the same time as the ones in Texas. From the late 1850s through the 1890s railroads were added piecemeal to the center of the country, with few reaching the coast. This was because the government did not want foreign soldiers to have the use of them in case of an invasion.

The rail system was much more efficient than the Göta Canal for sending goods across the country. The narrow canal could only handle small boats, and it was closed five months of the year due to snow and freezing conditions. A single steam locomotive could pull many freight cars and the rails could be cleared of snow and used year round.

However, the canal did provide a major stimulus to the Swedish manufacturing industry, which produced machinery needed to build the canal and then later was retooled to produce trains and associated equipment.

Swedish railroad building, late 1800s

My great-great grandfather (Carl August's father) was Carl Frederik Larsson, born in the early 1800s in Sweden. One of Mama's written stories is about Carl Larsson and his father Lars. She said that they lived in Östergötland near Omberg Mountain. Omberg is the tallest of a line of hills separating Lake Vättern from the plains of Östergötland. Lars had a mill on the Verland River. I have been unable to locate this river. Mama may have misspelled or misremembered the name. Or the name she heard might have been vrålande, a Swedish word that means "roaring or yelling." This could have been a local name applied to a noisy river. Because of the extreme variation in elevation in Sweden, the rivers are not always useful for navigation, but they are great for running mills.

View from Omberg, along Lake Vättern

Reconstructed water mill in Hunneberg, Sweden

According to Mama, when Lars' son Carl was a teenager, he moved in with the local doctor and was trained by him. The doctor sent Carl to the University at Uppsala to get a medical degree, but the old doctor's health failed and his income dropped before Carl's education was done. He was unable to maintain Carl's university fees, so Carl had to return home. Carl began treating local poor people for free.

A nearby baron's wife got sick and her physicians were unable to cure her. As a last resort, they called Carl, who cured the baroness with home grown herbs. In gratitude, the baron paid for the rest of Carl's university education in Germany. I cannot verify all the details of Mama's story, but our cousin Charles Carlson found the birth record for Carl August Carlson in Sweden. This document names Carl August's father as Carl Frederick Larsson. It appears that, like many of Mama's tales, there was at least a kernel of truth.

In many Swedish families, children's last names were "son" or "dotter" after their father's or mother's first names, so the concept of a family name was flexible. "Carl Larsson" fits Bell's recollection of an ancestor named Lars. The birth record cousin Charles found does not list Carl Larsson's occupation.

Several of Carl August's children were born in the province of Småland (meaning "many small lands") just south of Östergötland. The soil tends to be thin and rocky. About half the province is forested, and rich in lakes and bogs. Agriculture is not feasible except in limited areas, but where the soil can produce at all, Swedes grow oats, rye, potatoes, peppermint and pear trees.

Historically, Småland has been a province of small farmers struggling to make a living in poor soil. Those who survived were hardy and inventive. Smålanders are well known for being thrifty, in the same way as the Scots. The province was an extremely poor one in the 1800s, and many of the Swedes who came to the U. S. during the big wave of immigration came from Småland. The very first Swedes arriving in Texas in the 1840s were all Smålanders. Today, there is a large museum in Småland, called the House of Immigrants, dealing solely with the Swedes who left between 1846 and 1930. It has a research library where people can come to look for their Swedish ancestors.

Small farm in Småland, late 1800s

Smålanders are known for other things besides being frugal. Since the 1740s, Småland has been called the Swedish "Kingdom of Glass" because of its many glass factories. Linnaeus, the famous Swedish botanist, was born in Småland. Perhaps the county's most well known person is Ingvar Kamprad, the founder of IKEA. The children's' play area in IKEA stores is named Småland, in a kind of bilingual pun.

At least one other related Carlson came to America, besides my great grandfather Carl August. According to Mama, her father's great uncle, John Carlson (who must have been Carl Frederick Larsson's brother), owned a citrus farm in the early 1900s in what is now Hollywood, California. A photo in my album shows Annie and Frances Carlson picking oranges from a large tree on his farm. I have no other information on John Carlson.

Frances (great Aunt Ellen's daughter) and Great AuntAnnie, picking oranges in Hollywood

Carl August Carlson was a farmer, forester, and veterinarian. He was born in Östergötland in 1848 and died in 1915 in Bishop, Texas at age 67. In 1873 he married Mathilda (Matilda) Person (Persson, Pearson) also called Mathilda Josefina Margaretha Jonas-dotter. She was born in 1850, in Östergötland, and died in 1903 in Texas. Carl August and Matilda are both buried in the Lund Lutheran church cemetery. Their children were:

Carl Werner (Verner) 1874-1966. Born in Linderas, Småland, immigrated age 13, died age 82.
Anna Gunilla (Annie) 1876-1972. Born in Linderas, Småland, immigrated age 11, died age 96.
Carl Arvid 1879-1959. Born in Hult, Småland, immigrated age 9, died age 80.
Jennie Augusta 1880-1923. Born in Hult, Småland, immigrated age 10 or 11 (after the rest of the family), died age 43.
Ellen Matilda 1882-1964. Born in Hult, Småland, immigrated age 6, died age 87.
August Richard 1885-1973. Born in Vastra Ryd, Östergötland, immigrated age 3, died age 87.
Oscar Ivar 1890-1967. Born in Round Rock, Texas, died age 77.
Nina Elvira and Erik (maybe twins) born 1896 in Round Rock, Texas. Erik died as a toddler. Nina died in 1911, age 15.

Spelling was pretty flexible in the 1800s. "Carl" could be spelled with a C or a K. "Werner" in Swedish was pronounced with a V instead of a W, and this led to a spelling change in Werner's name.

There is some confusion about exactly when each Carlson family member arrived and in what order. Mama said that Carl August came first, then the oldest son Verner, then the rest of the family. Jenny, my cousin Swede's daughter, told me that according to her family stories, Arvid and Verner arrived in Texas at the same time. The dates in various sources are contradictory. But certainly by 1888 the entire family was in Texas.

Another confusing issue is that apparently the family came to New Jersey before Texas. Mama never told me this. Sue, however, remembers the story and says that Carl August was "recruited" in New Jersey by a Swede who was bringing Swedes to Texas.

Sue also remembers a story about one of the Carlson boys, but she is not sure which one it was. Looking at the Carlson sons' ages, the only one that might have fit the story was Verner. Arvid, the next younger boy, was five years younger and could not have traveled alone.

According to Sue's remembered story, Verner arrived in America on the east coast and was befriended by a Swede named Swenson, whom he called "Rik Swenson," meaning "rich Swenson." Rik Swenson convinced the Carlson lad to move to Texas, to a Swedish community. Verner had little money, but Rik Swenson paid his rail fare. To survive on the long train trip, Verner sold apples and hot coffee on the train. Somehow he managed a way to grind the beans and heat water. The profit he made allowed him to feed himself. This entire story may be erroneous, but I find it interesting that the "Rik" man in it had the same name as the famous Swenson who ran the Swedish pipeline to Texas.

Cousin Charles Carlson found the Record of Leaving for America document in Swedish records for the Carlson family emigration, dated June of 1888. It lists Carl August Carlsson, wife Matilda Jonsson, and children Annie, Arvid, Ellen and Richard. Verner and Jennie were not on that list.

Beth Boettcher gave me a copy of the Lund church registry for the Carlsons, dated 1901. The children included were Ellen, Richard, Oscar and Nina. That document has the family's arrival date as 1888, except for Jennie, who came in 1891, and the Persons, who came in 1895. I am pretty sure that some of these dates are wrong.

I believe that Verner, the oldest child, arrived first in Texas. *Swedes in Texas* says he arrived in Texas in 1887, the year before his parents. Verner went to work on a farm near Round Rock, which was then a fairly new Swedish community. This must have been arranged in advance of his arrival. It is possible that the family was

41

in New Jersey first, and Verner took a train to Texas. Probably we will never know the details.

Round Rock, blacksmith shop circa 1881, six years before Verner arrived

Jennie emigrated after the rest of the family, traveling with Matilda's parents Jonas and Anna Lisa Person. I don't know whether Carl August's parents were still alive at the time the family left Sweden.

My sister Sue told me that the family left Jennie behind in order to help the grandparents make the trip. This is an indication of just how children were considered an asset at the time, and how much responsibility was expected of them. Jennie was probably somewhere around 10 or 11 years old when she and her grand-parents left Sweden. It is interesting that the family chose Jennie to help the grandparents rather than Annie, who was four years older and might have been more assistance than Jennie. I assume it was because Annie was needed to help with Ellen and Richard, who were both pretty young.

Beth Boettcher gave me a copy of Carl August's citizenship certificate, dated 1894 and written in Williamson County, Texas. He swore his support of the Constitution, and promised to renounce any fidelity to the King of Sweden.

Many Swedes who emigrated had lived their entire lives in one small village or even on the same farm, so journey across the world seemed much more frightening. But our Carlson family had moved around, and the kids were born in various places in Småland and Östergötland. Swede's daughter Jenny pointed out that the varying birthplaces were probably a reflection of the family's custom of following the work. Carl August had several different types of jobs in agriculture, forest management, and timber production. Arvid told his grandchildren that for a while the family raised sheep. Apparently Arvid loathed sheep as a result of this experience. Verner also spoke of being a shepherd as a boy.

Carl August and the family first settled in Round Rock, where they were tenant farmers, not sharecroppers. The difference is that tenant farmers owned the crop and their own farming equipment. Sharecroppers owned neither the crop nor the farm equipment. They did not have as good a deal and did not have as much social standing as tenant farmers.

Carl rented land from the Nelsons, a well-known Swedish family from Smaland who settled in Brushy Creek in the 1850s. They changed their last name from Nilsson to Nelson when they immigrated. The patriarch, Arvid Nelson, started a trading business, hauling goods between central Texas and the coast. The family invested their profits in land. They bought thousands of acres, most of it around Brushy Creek (later called Round Rock).

Carl August Carlson

Arvid's son Andrew John Nelson (originally Anders Johan) eventually became one of the wealthiest men in Texas, second only to S. M. Swenson. Like Swenson, A. J. Nelson helped many Swedes to immigrate and sold or rented Texas farmland to Swedes. He made a lot of money during the Civil War, hauling timber and supplies for the Confederate Army. He wisely insisted on being paid in gold rather than Confederate paper scrip.

The Nelsons donated the bricks used to build Palm Valley Lutheran Church. The family had many tenant farmers working the land for them, including the Carlsons.

During the time when the Carlsons were renting from the Nelsons, three more children were born. Oscar came in 1890, and the twins, Nina and Erik arrived in 1896. Erik lived only a couple of years. Matilda was 46 when the twins were born. She had a hard time birthing Oscar when she was 40. I cannot imagine going through a pregnancy at age 46, and having twins!

In 1894, Carl August became a citizen. A. J. Nelson and N. Stark were his character witnesses. Both of them swore that Carl had been in the country for more than five years and that he was a man of good moral character. A. J. Nelson was, of course, the Swede from whom Carl and Verner rented land. I do not know who Mr. Stark was. Mr. Nelson died only a year after signing Carl August's papers.

In November of 1897 Carl August bought about 100 acres near the town of Elgin in the small community of Lund, in Bastrop County. Swede has a copy of the purchase papers, and made one for me.

Carl paid $450 down, and promised an additional $300 annually for ten years. Using an online inflation calculator, the total purchase price would be worth over $95,000 in today's money. He bought the land from George Washington Walling, Jr., a native of New Jersey who married a Texas farm girl and settled in Austin as an insurance agent. I am not sure how Mr. Walling acquired the land.

The picture below is one I took at the old Carlson farm in 2012.

By the late 1890s Lund had two cotton gins, a blacksmith shop, a school and a general store. Everything else the Carlsons needed was available six or eight miles away in Elgin, which was on the rail line. Those few miles were still a barrier to frequent visits, considering the mules could only pull their wagon about 3 mph. By 1900 Elgin had five cotton gins and three brick factories, and was becoming an important agricultural center in Bastrop County.

Lund's general store, photo from the 1930s.
The store opened in 1894. It was owned by a succession of Swedes until 1944.

*Swedes in Texas* has a listing of the eighty-five Swedish men (and a few widowed women) who were heads of households in Lund. A handful of these were dead by the time the book was printed, including Carl August Carlson and the long time blacksmith, Nels Ankarstolpe, who was struck by lightning and killed in 1914. I am not sure whether it was Ankarstolpe's work as the first Lund blacksmith or the unique method of his death that determined his inclusion in the book. He was an unmarried man, one of the few included. A young widow was praised for her ability to manage the farm after her husband was "badly beaten by a Negro, and died of his injuries." Some of the mini-biographies in the book made me want to know the rest of the story.

Except for the blacksmith, a couple of carpenters, the minister, a schoolteacher or two, and the folks who owned the cotton gins and store, all the Lund residents were farmers. Fifty-four of the eighty-five families were members of the Lutheran Church in Lund. By the time Carl August arrived there, it was not quite the wilderness that the earliest Lund settlers experienced. The community was tight-knit, and people helped each other. Swedish/Texan farm families lived in much the same way as they did in Sweden. As in Sweden, they attended church, celebrated traditional Swedish holidays, and helped each other build houses and barns and bring in the harvest.

Sometime after the purchase of the Lund farm in the fall of 1897, Carl August separated his family. He left his wife Matilda and their oldest son, Verner, in charge of the leased Round Rock farm. The 1900 census shows Verner as head of household in Round Rock. He was then twenty-five years old. Living with him were his mother Matilda, his sisters Annie, Ellen, Jennie, and Nina, and his Person grandparents.

Carl August, Arvid, Richard and Oscar are not in the census at all for 1900. They were helping their father build a house, dig a well, and plant cotton in Lund. The boys were still quite young. Arvid was eighteen, Richard was twelve, and Oscar was seven. But they were expected to work, and they did. In 1901 most of the family moved into the new Lund farmhouse and joined the Lund Lutheran church. Verner stayed in Round Rock and continued as a tenant farmer. Annie stayed with him for several years.

The family must have been affected by the Great Galveston Hurricane, which hit the coast in September of 1900. That storm was the biggest natural disaster in American history; it killed thousands of people and ruined crops in a two hundred mile swath all the way through the mid-western states. It hit Canada four days after decimating the Texas coast, and a few hundred people died in Canada. Most of the states' rice and cotton crops were lost. But the Carlsons survived and lived in Lund for many years.

My grandmother Ella Engblom's parents also farmed in the Lund area, as did her grandparents, the Westlings. The Carlson, Westling and Engblom families all attended the Swedish Evangelical Bethlehem Lutheran Church of Lund. Anders Engblom, my mother's maternal grandfather, was a charter member of the church in 1897. Mama told me that Anders, a carpenter, helped build the original church. This little church was where my grandparents Oscar and Ella were confirmed in the Lutheran faith. Oscar was confirmed in 1904, when he was fourteen years old.

The Lutheran Church was at the center of the community in Sweden, and it became so in America as well. Besides being a place of worship, it was the place where news was exchanged and important events (marriages, funerals, baptisms) celebrated. Church attendance was a way of maintaining one's Swedish cultural identity and language.

A handful of Swedish and Norwegian pastors founded the Lutheran Augustana College and Theological Seminary in 1860, in Wisconsin. Within about a decade the Seminary began turning out well-educated ministers, including Dr. John Stamline, who helped found the Lund church and years later, married my grandparents.

The original Lund church

In 1902 the Lund church commissioned a massive altar painting by a famous Swedish/American painter, Olof Grafström. The painting is the only one of Grafström's many altar paintings to have been put into a Texas church. It is a depiction of the Crucifixion, with a woman kneeling at the foot of the cross. The work cost the congregation about $150.00, most of which was raised by the Young People's Society. I would like to think that my grandparents Oscar and Ella participated in the fund raising. They would have been twelve and thirteen years old when the altar painting was installed. Certainly some of the older Carlson children would have participated. I imagine the altar painting is now worth a lot more than its original purchase price.

Altar and painting in the old Lund church

In 1924, the congregation had grown so much that a bigger church was built across the road. This newer building was demolished in a tornado in 1980. The church bell, the beloved altar painting, a few pews and some stained glass windows survived and were incorporated into the new building. This new church is an ordinary looking brick structure, which is a pity. The surrounding area has several old wooden Lutheran churches built in the late 1800s, and they have the more interesting traditional shape and appearance of a Swedish church. But the Lund church has survived time and calamities and still has a thriving congregation of mainly Swedish/Americans. And it has one advantage that the original church lacked: air conditioning.

In 1899, the Lund church established a six weeks summer Swedish language school. My grandfather Oscar (and probably his wife Ella) attended classes there. The summer Swedish school continued until 1923.

The Swedish language was retained in the Lund church longer than in most Texas Swedish churches. Starting in 1929 the number of English services was slowly increased over time, so that by the 1960s only one afternoon service was in Swedish. Now all the services are in English.

*Swedes in Texas in Words and Pictures*, 1918, describes Lund: "Lund is about eight miles northeast of Elgin in Travis County. It was uninhabited, forested prairie until the 1880s. When one of the area's first Swedes had bought land here, they said that he had settled outside the borders of civilization. But history repeats itself even in Lund. After only a few years and side by side with its mother community in an area that was forbidding there are now plowed and attractive fields with beautiful farms around a nice and suitable Lutheran country church. More Swedes moved here in the 1890s."

I love the description of the church as "nice and suitable." I think this is a way of saying that it was a small, modest church, and not fancy. It is typical of the time that farmed land, but not undeveloped land, was considered beautiful. Undeveloped fertile land was practically unknown in Sweden, and the immigrants probably did not appreciate the natural beauty of the untouched landscape as much as they did the "plowed and attractive fields."

The Lundgrens, another Swedish-American family, now own the old Carlson farm. The Lundgrens are descendants of Swedes who settled in Lund in the late 1800s, about the same time as the Carlsons.

The original Carlson house and other buildings are long gone, but Mrs. Lundgren has an old oval-framed photograph of the farmhouse and barn. The photo has some stains, scrapes and other damage, but you can make out the house to the right, a barn and another outbuilding to the left, and in the center a team of four mules being held by a man, probably Carl. The fact that Carl August paid money to have his home photographed with mules, barn and wagon says a lot about his pride in being a farm owner.

Cousin Swede kindly held up the framed picture, and I photographed it with my little digital camera. Later, I cropped and enlarged the picture so that only Carl August, two mules and the house show.

The house looks small by today's standards, but it is neat and attractive, and there are trees planted around it. There is a front porch running the width of the house, and all the windows are framed with decorative shutters. A shaded porch was an essential addition. During the day, the Texas sunshine heated up the house, and cooking on a wood stove made it worse. My grandfather told me of sleeping on the porch in the summer.

Color photography did not exist when this picture was made, so the photo was hand tinted. Most of the colors have faded, although the red of the barn is still clear. Green-painted leaves on the trees have become a light teal. The house was probably nicer and newer than any the family had in Sweden, and was certainly built in a different style.

Back in Sweden, farmhouses required steep roofs to shed heavy winter snows. They were built with thick logs, for better insulation from the cold and to support the massive roofs. They were designed for a cold climate and heavy snows.

Typical Swedish log farmhouse, late 1800s

The earliest Swedish Texans built small log homes made from whatever local trees could be chopped down. But for the later immigrants to Texas, there were enough available sources for milled lumber, nails, and roofing materials to build a frame house. The Carlson house was typical of the farmhouses being built in Texas at that time. We saw many beautiful examples of old frame houses in the Lund and Elgin area.

I don't know how many bedrooms were in the house, but I am sure there were not enough for everyone to have a separate one. In 1901, the household included ten people: Carl August and Matilda, Matilda's parents, Ellen, Richard, Oscar, Nina, Jennie and Arvid. Annie had finished midwifery school, and lived in Round Rock with Verner.

Like most Lutherans, the family took Sunday as a day of rest and religious observation. But every other day was a day of work, and all the children were expected to do their part. Carl August worked the farm, but also made some money as a veterinarian for neighboring farmers. The family had a vegetable garden, some chickens, mules or horses and sometimes a cow or two. Fishing and hunting contributed to the household economy.

Matilda died at the farm in 1903, at age 53. She was able to enjoy the new farmhouse and perhaps a slightly better lifestyle for only a few years. Her death certificate says she died of "cardiac asthenia," with contributing factors being "rheumatism" and "chronic constipation." Cardiac asthenia means literally "heart weakness." It is not a recognized condition in modern medicine. I think it is likely that she had a heart attack. I cannot imagine that rheumatism (joint pain) contributed to her death, but constipation might have. Straining while having a bowel movement can trigger a heart attack in someone with a pre-existing heart condition. Matilda was laid to rest in the Lund church cemetery, the first of the Carlson family to be buried there. Nina was only seven years old when her mother died, and Oscar, the next oldest, was thirteen. The rest of the family pulled together to parent the two youngest ones.

The 1910 census shows Carl August still living at the Lund farm with Jennie, Richard, Oscar, Nina, and the Persons, who were 89 and 91. Under "occupation" all of Carl's sons are called farm laborers. Oscar had just graduated from Trinity Lutheran College in Round Rock, but apparently had not yet found a job. The occupation for Carl's daughters and in-laws is written as "none." I suspect this was not quite accurate, since somebody had to do the laundry, cleaning, cooking, feed the chickens and work the vegetable garden.

Nina died of a "fever" in 1911 and was buried next to her mother. Her loss was another terrible blow to the family. I don't know what caused the fever. The Carlson graves in the Lund church cemetery have modest markers. I am not sure who paid to have them installed.

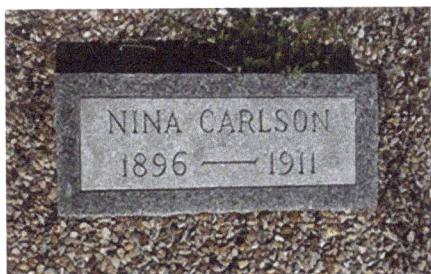

In 1913, the family moved to another farm in Bishop, Texas, and Carl died two years later, at age 67. I was unable to find his death certificate or cause of death.

By the time Carl August passed on, Ellen and Arvid were both married and living elsewhere. Oscar was working in a bank in Kenedy. He never had an interest in farming as an occupation, although he loved to garden.

Verner, Richard, Annie and Jennie lived together on the Bishop farm for a few years after Carl died. In 1919 or 1920, Annie moved to Austin to live with Ellen, who was widowed in 1919. Jennie lived with her two brothers and kept house for them until she died of cancer in 1923.

*Swedes in Texas in Words and Pictures*, 1918, gives this account of Carl August Carlson's life:

> When this veterinarian passed away, one of the well-known and respected Swedes in Williamson and Travis counties in Texas was lost. He was born in Ekebyborna parish, Östergötland, emigrated with his wife and came to the United States and arrived in New Jersey in 1885. He did different types of manual labor there. He got sun-stroke and had to seek a different climate.
>
> In 1886 he came to Round Rock, Texas. He worked as a farmer but was often in demand as a veterinarian. In 1900 he moved to Lund, Texas, and lived there on his farm until 1913 when he moved to a new settlement in Bishop, Texas. After two years he died there in 1915. He was buried in the Lund cemetery, where his wife had been buried twelve years before her husband.
>
> Mrs. Carlson, born Mathilda Person, was also from Östergötland, and born in Åsbo parish. The couple had these children: Verner, Anna, Arvid, Jennie, Elin, Richard and Oscar. Two children, Nina and Erik, are dead.
>
> Dr. Carlson and his family belonged to the Lutheran Church in Lund and they took an active role in the work.
>
> Mr. Carlson had further education than elementary school in Sweden. He went to a private school run by Countess Reutherskold; went to agricultural college, and attended the forestry training school at Anneherg. He was then forest-keeper for Baron Hermelin on a large manor estate in Östergötland. He also attended veterinary school. For a few years before he went to America, he was the head supervisor at a large sawmill. He was involved in some speculative ventures and suffered heavy losses. Mr. Carlson, like many others, then decided to immigrate to America.

I cannot believe that Carl August came to central Texas to avoid another sunstroke! He must not have known what the Texas climate was like.

Countess Reutherskold and Baron Hermelin mentioned were members of historically well-known Swedish noble families. I was unable to find out anything about the Countess' private school, but there were hundreds of small private schools across Sweden at the time.

I am not sure where Carl August attended agricultural college. There were twenty-five Swedish agricultural schools in the mid to late 1800s, most of them in southern provinces. The young men they trained could go on to manage their own farms or supervise the farming on a large estate.

Carl August likely did not graduate from veterinary school, or the *Swedes in Texas* article would have mentioned it. But he certainly learned enough to help keep his neighbors' and his own farm animals healthier. Some people called him "Doctor Carlson" in recognition of his skills as a veterinarian. He may have learned some veterinary medicine as part of his agricultural school curriculum.

When Carl was studying forestry, Sweden was just beginning to realize the importance of managing its forests, which were the source of much of the country's income. In the early to mid 1800s Sweden exported a lot of timber, and burned tons of wood to melt metal ores. It was 1886 before the government enacted laws conserving forests. They were the first such laws in Europe. However, the management of forests was of interest to the Swedish Crown long before that. The depletion of national forests was a real threat, and might have led to a dire situation if the Crown had not intervened with numerous regulations on cutting.

In 1828 the Royal Institute of Forestry (Kungliga Skogsinstitutet) was established in Stockholm. Given Sweden's extensive forests, forestry study was an obvious choice for Carl, a smart young man hoping to ensure his continued employability.

Besides the Royal Forest Institute in Stockholm, there were six satellite forestry schools. The course of study at the Stockholm forestry school lasted two years, and the satellite schools offered training for a year. I have been unable to find any information about a forestry school or any other place in Sweden called "Anneherg," mentioned in *Swedes in Texas* as the place where Carl studied forestry.

However, among the six Swedish forestry schools was one in Hunneberg, in Västra Götaland County, on the other side of Lake Vättern from Östergötland, and just south of Lake Vänern. Hunneberg was probably where Carl studied forestry. It is a forested "tableland" mountain, today one of many national "ecoparks" in Sweden.

The curriculum required for Carl was rigorous. It included natural history, forest biology, tree planting, insect identification, mathematics, surveying, hunting, forest regulations, and map making.

Hunneberg tableland

The Hermelin family manor and forest property where Carl worked was in Ödeshög municipality, in Östergötland, about 35 miles from Carl's birthplace. Samuel Hermelin was the Baron at the time Carl worked as the Hermelin forest keeper. This job probably involved helping choose which trees to cut and managing the steam-powered sawmill.

The Hermelin family's only real claim to fame (besides employing my great grandfather) is that Samuel's son Eric Hermelin, born in 1860, was a famous Swedish author who translated Persian literature into Swedish. He was a brilliant but unstable man with a drinking problem, and spent most of his later years in a lunatic asylum in Lund, Sweden. When I read about this I wondered briefly whether Lund's lunatic asylum was the inspiration for naming Lund, Texas. Then I read that the town was named because Lund, Sweden is so famous. It has Sweden's oldest cathedral and second oldest university. I actually liked the lunatic asylum idea a bit better.

The sawmill failure and "speculative ventures" that brought financial losses to Carl August were probably due to a worldwide economic depression beginning in 1873 and lasting through 1879.

I am not sure where the family raised sheep, but I think it may have been in Vastra Ryd, Östergötland, where Richard was born. My reasoning is that both Arvid and Verner spoke about herding sheep as boys. They would have been about the right age for helping watch the sheep. The family lived in Vastr Ryd at least three years before emigrating. During that period, Richard was eleven to thirteen years old, and Arvid was six to nine years old.

The family probably did not make much money raising sheep. In Sweden sheep farming has never been a strong industry. Almost no wool was being exported from Sweden in the late 1800s. The native sheep have been a source of coarse wool and food for centuries. They are tough enough to stay outside in the winter, unlike the wimpier British sheep, which require shelter from snow. Unfortunately, the native sheep wool is not as fine as merino wool derived from sheep in Great Britain, New Zealand and Australia. All varieties of sheep are prone to attacks by Swedish wolves, lynx and bears and so require constant watching.

Arvid hated sheep so much that his family teased him about it. I assume this was in part due to their almost unbelievably stupid behavior. They will follow another sheep right off a cliff. They easily wander away and get lost from the herd. When a predator appears, they run in circles and panic. I understand Arvid's prejudice against sheep. Modern Swedish sheep farmers have started adding alpacas to their herds. The alpacas are smarter than sheep, and will fight off predators. There have been recent protests against this strategy, because people are afraid the elegant and intelligent guardian alpacas will be injured in the line of duty. Nobody seems to care about the sheep getting eaten.

# The Carlson Children

Carl Werner Carlson (Verner) was Carl and Matilda's first child, born in 1874 in Linderås, Småland, Sweden where Carl was working one of his many different jobs. Verner's birthplace is a town about 80 kilometers south of Ekebyborna, where his father was born. In 1924, Verner married Frances Melinda Henson. They had two sons, Carl Verner Carlson (1925-2002) and John Elmer Carlson (1928-1976).

Verner around 1914

In one of Mama's essays she describes Verner's trip to America. She said he came across the Atlantic by himself at age twelve or thirteen. Verner promised his mother to take off his winter underwear on the journey to America. She was afraid he would catch a chill. But on the ship, the weather got warmer and warmer and he got smellier and more uncomfortable. He was afraid to break his promise, so he suffered until the crewmembers held him down, stripped off his clothing, and tossed the underwear in the ocean.

My sister Sue wrote a poem in college, entitled, "The Ballad of Great Uncle Verner's Red Woolen Under Drawers." She won a prize for the poem. Apparently Verner enjoyed the poem immensely.

Mama said in her essay that Verner took a Swedish ship to New York and an American vessel to Galveston. From there he rode a train to Round Rock. His father had arranged for a job, which included room and board, a small salary and two sets of work clothes. Verner spoke no English, and was very shy. His mother wrote his name and destination on a handkerchief in India ink and sewed it in his jacket in case he got lost. He was expected to do a man's work. Fortunately, he was strong and large for his age. Mama said that he was already six feet tall at age twelve.

Sue remembers being told that Verner took a train from New York or New Jersey all the way to Texas, with no additional boat trip to Galveston.

According to Verner's grandson, John Randall Farmacka, Verner made illegal beer and sold it during Prohibition. John posted this interesting tidbit on Ancestry.com free pages. He had heard it from Louis Farmacka, one of Verner's neighbors and a family member by marriage. (Louis married Verner's stepdaughter and adopted Verner's grandson John Randall.) I know that my grandfather Oscar made beer. He talked about the bottles in his basement exploding from gas pressure in the Texas heat. Many of the Swedes in Texas made their own beer during Prohibition.

According to Bell, Verner fought in WW I. I have a photo that Bell said was Verner and his brother Richard in their uniforms. However, Richard's son Charles says his dad was never in the service, and the 1930 census says that Verner was not a veteran. So I am not sure who these two good-looking men might be, in the old photograph. They might be Engbloms, or they might be friends of the family.

I did locate (online) Verner's draft registration card, dated September 18, 1918. His signature from that card is below, proof that people of his generation were taught good penmanship. He was 44 years old, and the card states that he had gray eyes and blonde hair. Draft cards did not record exact height and weight, but the check marks indicate that he was tall with a medium build. The next of kin listed was his brother Oscar, in Kenedy Texas.

From *Swedes in Texas in Words and Pictures*, 1918:

CARL VERNER CARLSON is from Linderås, Småland, where he was born in 1874, and he came to Round Rock, Texas, in 1887. Mr. Carlson, who is unmarried, farms with his brother and sisters, Richard, Anna and Jenny. He was a tenant farmer on the Nelson estate in Williamson County for about twenty-five years. Mr. Carlson's parents were Dr. C. A. Carlson and his wife, Mathilda. His father died in Bishop, Texas, in December 1915, and his mother died in Lund, Travis County, in October 1903. Like their parents, they are members of the Swedish Lutheran congregation in Bishop, Texas. They take an active part in the congregation.

The Nelson estate mentioned here was that of A. J. Nelson, the same man who witnessed Carl August's citizenship papers and who rented land to Carl August as well.

Verner was a handsome man (like most Swedish men) who wore a big moustache. Verner grew the mustache to cover his crooked front teeth and had it his entire life. He married late in life (age 53). According to his grand daughter Peggy McManus, he was a wonderful man with a great sense of humor. His grandchildren called him PawPaw. In most of his photographs he is wearing suspenders.

Verner, like his siblings, loved fishing. The photograph below, from Peggy's family album, shows he had some bragging rights.

Mama said, in a 1996 letter to Peggy, that Verner was "one of the finest men to walk the earth." Mama told my brother Jerry that Verner was approved for a tractor loan when he was well past retirement age. Similarly, she got a new car loan in her eighties. Maybe Swedes are generally good credit risks, even in old age.

My older siblings all loved Verner. My brother Jerry told me that Uncle Verner reminded him of our brother Carl, who is also a tall, fine example of Swedish manhood. (Well, Carl is half Swedish, anyway). Sue remembers that as a child, she drew a picture of Verner and was particularly proud of getting his classic mustache right.

Until 1912, Verner was a tenant farmer for the Nelsons, north of Round Rock. In 1913 Verner, his father Carl, and his siblings Richard, Annie and Jennie moved to a new farm in Bishop Texas, thirty miles southwest of Corpus Christi in Nueces County, Texas. This county is in southeastern Texas on the Gulf of Mexico, and is part of the Texas Coastal Prairies region. The soil in some parts of the county is loamy and makes good farmland. I am not sure what precipitated the move, but Bishop was a brand new town and had been heavily advertised to central Texas farmers. They might have got a good price on the property.

Bishop was a planned community built next to the railroad. The developer, F. Z. Bishop, laid out business, residential and farm tracts in 1910. He included sewage and water systems, sidewalks, streets, a telephone system, an electric power plant, a store and a hotel. By 1913, when the Carlsons moved there, what had been undeveloped scrub and cactus was becoming a relatively prosperous and modern farming community. By 1921 Bishop was called the "Cotton Capital of the Coast." The Great Depression hit the community hard, and many residents left. It is still a very small town today, and the primary business is still agriculture, but the building of a chemical plant in the 1940s was a boost to employment.

1910 photograph of Bishop

In 1924 both Verner and Richard, who had been living together, married. They separated households after taking wives, but both continued farming. Verner married Frances Melinda (Linnie) Henson, a Swedish/American widow. She had two mostly grown sons and two small daughters, Marie and Irene. Her previous husband's name was Tipton.

Verner and Frances wedding photograph, 1924, with the two little girls, Marie and Irene Tipton.

I think having the girls in the wedding picture is a strong indication of Verner's affection for them.

Verner's farmhouse in Bishop, where Carl, Jr. was born in 1925.

A year after they married, Verner and Frances had the first of their two sons. The year after that, in 1926, they moved to a farm close to Agua Dulce, between the towns of Alice and Corpus Christi. They farmed there for twenty-two years, until Verner became blind at age 74. The cause of his blindness might have been cancer, since two of his grandchildren reported that. But my sister Sue recalls he had glaucoma. It is possible that he had both.

Sue remembers the Agua Dulce farm from the early 1940s. Verner grew sorghum in one field, and supplied some to Sue's pet rabbits. Charles, Richard's son, fondly remembers visiting the farm also.

Agua Dulce is a very small town today, and it was even smaller in the 1920s. The settlement was fairly new when Verner moved there, but it had the three essentials for farmers at the time: a general store, cotton gin, and a blacksmith. The settlement was named for the Agua Dulce (sweet water) Creek, site of a famous battle during the Texas revolution against Mexico. The nearby (much larger) town of Alice is famous for being the birthplace of Tejano music in the 1940s.

Verner and his two step-daughters with the farm horse circa 1926, near Agua Dulce.

1927 photo of Verner and his brother Richard.

In 1948, when Verner lost his vision, he and Frances moved to an apartment in Corpus Christi, about 40 miles from the Agua Dulce farm. Verner lived to be 92, and Frances died at 81. I was unable to locate Verner's death certificate. Frances died of "circulatory collapse and hypertensive heart disease."

My parents spent the night at the Agua Dulce farm one night, and they heard Verner get up in the middle of the night to wind the hall clock, which normally chimed every hour. He had missed his usual clock winding time because of having company. Verner woke up because the clock did not chime. The family thought it was funny that Verner's sleep was interrupted because of the absence of a sound.

## Verner's Children

Carl Verner Carlson Jr. (1925-2002), married Reta Adams and had four daughters. He was an oilfield consultant. I found an email address for his daughter Peggy and sent an email to her in September 2013, inquiring about whether she was interested in exchanging family information. She was kind enough to respond with both stories and pictures. It turned out that she had been in correspondence with my mother years earlier.

Carl Verner, Jr. joined the army when he was eighteen, two years after the Second World War began. The Army sent him to various bases in Florida and Mississippi. He was trained as a medic and shipped to France and then to Germany. In 1945 he was wounded while caring for another wounded man. He was in the war zone for such a short time that he never had a chance to get a bath or even change his clothes! Carl got a Purple Heart.

Carl Verner, Jr., and Carl Verner Sr., around 1943.

64

Carl, Reta and their girls

Verner's other son, John Elmer Carlson (1928-1976) was married twice and had two sons. I don't know happened to his wives. He gave up custody of his sons and a different family adopted each boy.

Marie (Frances' daughter by her first husband) and her husband Louis Farmacka adopted the oldest boy, John Randall (Randy) Carlson (1951-2008), who served in the Marines and was a police officer after he got out.

Randy posted some family information online a couple of years before he died. He said that John Elmer, his father, was murdered while working as a cab driver in Des Moines. He hinted that John Elmer was an alcoholic, which is perhaps why the boys were adopted out. Peggy McManus confirmed this and said that Randy was also an alcoholic. My sister Sue remembers that John Elmer was a problem child and had to be bailed out of jail periodically.

Randy wrote on Rootsweb.com that he grew up in South Texas and heard four different languages until he was about 10. His grandfather Verner spoke Swedish, his adoptive father Louis Farmacka spoke Czech, the farmhands spoke Spanish, and most everyone else spoke English. He remembered Verner (after he lost his sight) reminiscing about his days as a shepherd boy in Sweden. John had the idea that the Carlsons left Sweden for more religious freedom. I had not heard this before.

John Randall (Carlson) Farmacka, when he was a police officer in Tennessee

A family named Stanfield adopted John Elmer's younger boy, Carl Dale Carlson (1952-1975). I know nothing about him, his adoptive family, or why he died so young. He served in the Navy.

Carl Dale (Carlson) Stanfield

Peggy Mc Manus wrote me the following: "I don't know if you knew or not but my grandfather Carl Verner Sr. went blind somewhere around the age of 74. I was told it was from a cancer in the eye but I really don't know for sure since he was completely blind in both eyes. My oldest sister is the only one of us four girls he ever was able to see but he knew us all by feeling our hair and face when we'd sit down beside him. Also, as far as I know, he never was in the war so it will be interesting to see that picture of him in uniform. My parents always talked about what an honest honorable man he was and that he hated drinking so I'd be surprised if it were him who was selling illegal beer but of course I wouldn't know for sure."

Peggy and I surmise that the reason Verner hated drinking is that he saw how damaging it was to his own family. Neither of us is sure about the veracity of John's claim that Verner made beer during prohibition (1920-1933).

My sister Sue told me that our grandfather Oscar refused a job as a Federal Agent in the 1920s once he found out he was supposed to inform on all the Swedes in the local community who were involved in bootlegging. Some of them were his relatives and in-laws.

Verner and Frances in their later years. His moustache looks the same.

Anna Gunilla Carlson (Annie) was the second Carlson child, born in Linderås, Smaland, two years after her brother Verner. She died in Round Rock in 1972, at age 96. She was a midwife who delivered over 4,000 babies in her lifetime.

Annie around 1914

Annie got her diploma from the Chicago Midwife Institute in 1899, when she was twenty-three years old. The school Annie attended was an excellent one, and probably cost the family a fair bit of money for tuition, room and board. The training required about ten months to complete. She had already been helping deliver babies in Texas, working as an assistant to a physician.

The Illinois State Board of Health inspected the Chicago Midwife Institute in 1897 and found that it was well equipped and provided the proper instruction required for midwives. The Board voted to accept certificates issues by the Institute. This was during a time when Chicago had over a dozen schools for medicine, nursing and midwifery, and some of them were fraudulent or poorly run. The state cracked down after a series of scandals. Fortunately, Annie attended one of the best schools available.

In her early practice, Annie got around by horse, and delivered babies in homes with no indoor plumbing and no other assistance other than the new mother's immediate family. In those days a midwife stayed after the delivery until she was sure the mother and baby were doing well, the house was tidy, and there was someone to cook and clean for the new mom. Almost all babies were born at home with midwife attendants. Annie's clients were predominantly, but not exclusively Swedish. For a recently immigrated woman in labor, I imagine it was a great comfort to have a birth attendant who spoke the same language.

Annie lived in Bishop, Texas with her father, brother and sisters from 1913 until 1919 or 1920. Then she moved to Austin and lived with her sister Ellen, who was widowed and needed help raising her five children and running a boarding house.

While the rest of the family was in Bishop and Oscar was in Kenedy, Annie wrote him a card, sent to his bank address. I cannot accurately read everything she wrote, but the word "broder" (brother) is in the salutation, and she signed it "Anna." Using an online translator, and magnifying the image, I was able to decipher some words. It appears she says all in the family are healthy, and that perhaps they will visit Corpus Christi. She also says the cotton crop is beautiful, shining in the sun. Many of the words are not translatable because I cannot read her handwriting.

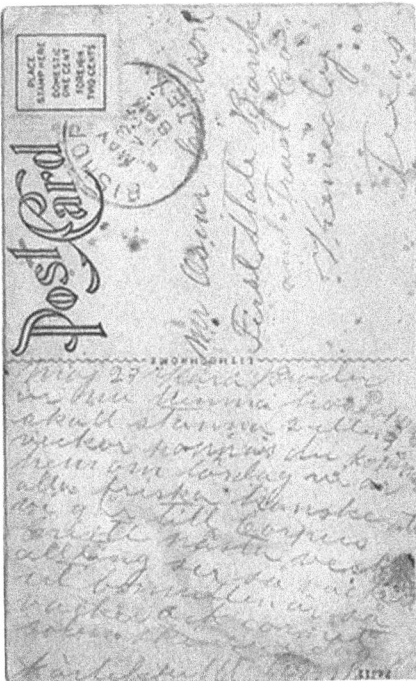

Bacjk of postcard to Oscar from Annie, 1914.

69

The picture on Annie's postcard to Oscar is of Bishop, Texas, where most of the rest of the family was living.

In an interview by the Austin newspaper when she was 86, Annie explained why midwives always asked for water to be heated. It was to bathe the baby. There were no automatic hot water heaters in homes then.

For much of her life, Annie lived with her sister Ellen, and helped raise Ellen's children, with whom she was very close. Annie had a career at a time when most American women did not have that choice. One reason for this was her family's support of her goals, but also because she was such a strong minded person. I greatly admire Annie's dedication to her profession. I think she would enjoy knowing that midwifery is making a comeback in this country.

Between 1910 and 1930 the medical profession tried to eliminate midwives entirely. They were unsuccessful. Annie's midwifery practice ended because of her own advancing age and because more women were choosing hospital, doctor-assisted births. By the onset of WW II, when Annie was sixty-five, fewer than half of all Texas births were attended by midwives

Annie and Oscar in Corpus Christi, 1938.

Annie worked with a very well known Austin physician, Dr. Joe Gilbert (1873-1951). He referred patients to her for uncomplicated births, and she called in the doctor when there was a problem. Dr. Gilbert was the founder of the U. T. Student Health Center and helped found two Austin hospitals. While Annie was working as a midwife, Dr. Gilbert was director of the Student Health Service, health officer for the city of Austin, and a practicing surgeon. They had a relationship based on mutual trust, and Dr. Gilbert did not suffer from the general physicians' distrust of midwives.

ANNIE CARLSON REMEMBERS 4,000 BABIES
Midwife explains the need for hot water.

Annie in 1982, from a newspaper article about her career as a midwife.

My cousin Swede Carlson told me that at Annie's funeral, the Lutheran minister asked everyone who had been delivered by Annie to stand up. More than half the people stood.

Mama told me that a farmhand raped Annie when she was a teenager, and her brothers and father caught and quietly hanged the man responsible. I have grave doubts about this story, but Mama said the rape was why Annie never married. Possibly it was so traumatic it prevented her from wanting marriage, but at the time a non-virginal woman was not considered a good candidate for the position of wife. Werner's granddaughter, Peggy Mc Manus, said

71

that her mother also told her that Annie was raped. She did not hear that anyone was hanged for it. Maybe Mama added that part.

Annie spent the last six years of her life in the Trinity Lutheran Home, in Round Rock. It was on the site of what had been Trinity Lutheran College. She died of arteriosclerotic heart disease.

Carl Arvid Carlson was Carl and Matilda's third child. He was born in 1879, three years after Annie. When Arvid arrived, the family was living near Hult, Småland, a small port town on Lake Vänern.

In 1908 he married Amelia Johnson (1888-1974). Their children were:

Hildred Stotts 1909-2000
Helen Boettcher 1910-2000
Arvie Carl 1912- 2000
Evelyn 1915-1934
Roland 1918-1997

Swede Carlson, Roland's son, told me that Arvid was musically talented, and had learned violin in Sweden. He loved singing, and often played a "juice harp." A juice harp (also called jaws harp or Jews harp) is a very simple and ancient type of instrument. It is simply a reed stuck into a framework, and played using both mouth and hands.

He was compulsively neat in keeping his tools and important papers orderly. Arvid gave regular haircuts to his children and the neighbors. One Sunday a month was Haircut Day. When his son Roland came home for a visit after he was grown, Arvid was shocked at the terrible haircut someone else had given him, so he re-cut Roland's hair. This general tidiness and attention to detail was an integral part of his personality.

Arvid was an avid fisherman and liked to take his family camping and fishing. They fished with nets and seines as well as poles. He would bring home the fish in Number 3 washtubs, call the neighbors and give away what they could not eat.

Arvid loved the sport of boxing. He taught the basics to both his boys, and Arvie went on to fight professionally. Roland was a boxer also, but instead of fighting, he trained other boxers.

Like my grandfather Oscar and their brother Richard, Arvid was an alcoholic. He came home one night drunk, and ran his buggy into a train. The horse was killed, but luckily Arvid survived. His daughter Hildred would break or empty any whiskey bottles she found hidden. She once found a whiskey bottle in the hay, as she was watching Arvid and Arvie break a horse. She bashed the bottle on a fence post. This made Arvid really angry, partly because whiskey was so expensive. My mother and Richard's son Charles did the same thing when they found their fathers' hidden alcohol stashes.

Arvid made wine from the dark purple mustang grapes that grew wild around the farm. His grandson Swede also tried making wine with these grapes. He told me that a lot of sugar (2 or 3 pounds per gallon) must be added to the juice, since the grapes never get really sweet. But the wine was probably fairly good, and people in Texas still harvest mustang grapes for wine and jam. Sometimes homemade mustang grape wine gets up to 18% alcohol, so it can have quite a kick.

Arvid grew broomcorn (a variety of sorghum) in Lund. He harvested and dried the broomcorn, then made brooms, which he then took around to all the local stores to sell. Arvid also helped farm the nearby land belonging to his in-laws, the Johnsons, who were neighbors of the Carlsons.

Benjamin Franklin introduced broomcorn to the Americans in the 1700s. In 1810 a foot pedal broom-making machine was invented, and as a result, broom making became an important industry in the U. S. during the 19th century. Most broomcorn is now grown in Mexico.

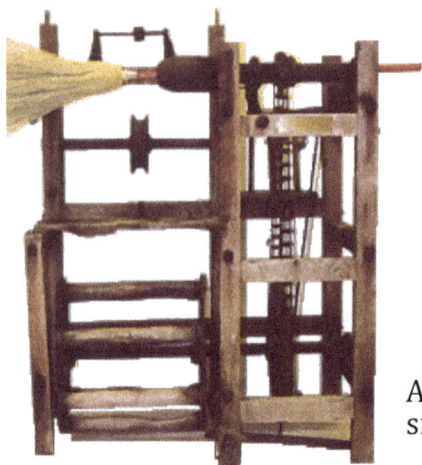
A foot pedal broom-making machine, similar to Arvid's.

Betty Lundgren, current owner of the old Carlson farm in Lund, remembers sweeping with Arvid's brooms. I have a suspicion that his brooms were more efficient than modern brooms with plastic bristles. Arvid's brooms also had the advantage of being biodegradable.

Arvid's WW I draft card says he was tall, with a slender build, red hair and grey eyes. He had the same lovely penmanship as the rest of the Carlson boys.

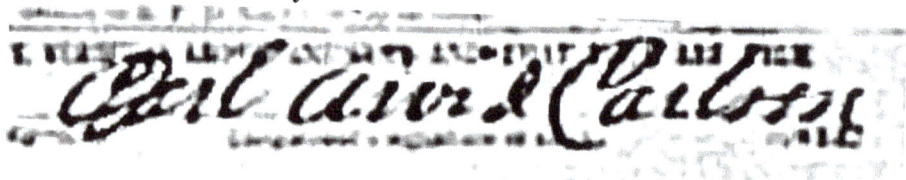

Arvid married a beautiful Swedish American woman, Amelia Johnson, who lived on an adjacent farm. Family lore says that he met Amelia when she was ten years old and he was twenty, and jokingly told her that he would marry her when she was old enough. He did marry her, and they had the first of five children when she was twenty-one. Amelia's name is also spelled "Emelia" in some of the old records, and Arvid called her "Meelie." Arvid's children called him "Papa" and his grandchildren called him "Farfar," Swedish for grandfather. Arvid died at age 80, of atherosclerotic heart disease. Amelia died of a heart attack at age 86.

Arvid and Amelia's wedding photograph.

*Swedes in Texas*, 1918, had this to say about the Johnson family and Arvid:

Mrs. CARL ALBERT JOHNSON was born in 1856, in Järstad parish, Östergötland, and immigrated to America in 1884. She first came to Oakland, Nebraska. In 1887, she married Carl Albert Johnson, who died in 1905.

Their children's names are: Amelia, Carl, Roland, Robert and Hulda. The Johnson family leased land around Hutto, Texas for many years; bought land around Lund community in 1896. Here Mrs. Johnson now lives.

ARVID CARLSON is the son of the well-known veterinary, Mr. Carl August Carlson, who came to this country in 1885 and to Texas in the following year. Arvid Carlson was born in Hult parish, Småland, in 1878, and he immigrated to the United States and to Round Rock, Texas, in 1888. He came to Lund, Texas, in 1897, where his father had bought land. In 1908 he married Emelia Johnson, daughter of the late Albert Johnson, in Lund. She was born in Hutto, Texas, in 1888. Four nice children are a pleasure to the couple: Hildred, 1909, Helen, 1910, Arvie, 1912, and Evelyn, 1915. Mr. Carlson has a pleasant and friendly nature and sees the future in a positive light. The family belongs to the Lutheran Church in Lund.

From the things I have been told by his family, I have pieced together a picture of Arvid's personality. He was a generous man, and very cheerful, although he grieved terribly and was depressed when his young daughter Evelyn committed suicide. Arvid loved his wife and children. According to Swede, the "pleasant and friendly nature" described in the *Swedes of Texas* book was accurate. As a child, Swede never saw Arvid angry, nor did he ever see his grandmother "Meelie" show any temper. This was a stark contrast to my own grandfather Oscar, who was famous in our immediate family for getting spitting mad and yelling.

Arvid may have been a gentle man, but he was not a wimp. He certainly did not tolerate any threats to his family. Several stories by Tina Boettcher (one of Arvid's grand daughters) are printed in *Elgin, Etc., Stories of Elgin Texas*, published in 2008 by the Elgin Historical Association. Tina wrote about the time (around 1915) that local members of the KKK visited Arvid. She heard this story from her mother Helen and her uncle Arvie.

The men, on horseback and dressed in their white robes and hoods, came to warn Arvid about having black friends. He had been tipped off in advance that they were coming. He told his wife and small children to get under the table and went outside to meet the riders, carrying his loaded shotgun. Little Arvie disobeyed and watched from a window.

Arvid recognized two of the men by their boots. He called them by name and said he would shoot them first if there were any trouble. The riders said their piece and left. The next morning, Arvid dressed up in his church clothes, stuck a pistol in his belt, rode into Elgin and called on the families of the two men he had recognized. He told them if the men came around his farm again, he would shoot them. Then he went to the sheriff and pressed charges. One of the two men left town. The other went to prison, but in a typically Texas twist, he was hired as a law enforcement officer after he served his time. I assume the rest of the KKK-ers went about their lives as usual.

# Arvid's Children

Hildred, Helen and Evelyn all went to nursing school in Austin. Tragically, Evelyn committed suicide in 1937, after only four months of school. Swede and Charles B. told me that Evelyn was despondent over a boyfriend. She was only nineteen years old. Beth Boettcher gave me a copy of Evelyn's newspaper obituary, which is heart breaking. The article does not mention a boyfriend, but instead says that Evelyn had suffered from ill health and had to leave nursing school. She had an operation on her ear, after which she suffered from severe headaches. She was so despondent over her health that she killed herself with a shotgun blast to the chest, while in her bedroom. Her mother, hearing the sound, rushed in. The girl was still alive, but barely. Amelia ran to a neighbor for help, and a doctor was called. She was taken by ambulance to Austin, and a blood transfusion was attempted, but Evelyn could not be saved.

Hildred finished nursing school and worked as a nurse with the WPA near Austin. She married Frank Stotts, and had one child, a daughter named Frances Ann (b 1939). According to Swede, Frances disappeared in the 1960s, and was never found. Her boyfriend was overheard telling someone that he had killed the girl, but there was never enough evidence to prosecute. Hildred spent her life searching futilely for her missing child. She died in Albuquerque in 2000.

As a nursing student, Helen was rooming in Austin with Martha Mazoch, and introduced Martha to her brother Roland ("Big Swede"). They eventually married.

After graduating as a nurse, Helen married one of her patients, a wealthy German/American named Clemens John Boettcher, who was 34 years older. Clem and Helen had two children, Charles Frederick Boettcher (born 1941) and Clementine (Tina) Helen Hollingsworth (born 1942). Clem died not live long after their second child was born. Helen married a second time in

1945 to Jerry John Stach (1907-1970). They had no children. Helen died in Elgin in 2000.

Charles and his wife Beth live in East Bernard, Texas. They have two children, Jerry Clem and Brenda Beth, and seven grandchildren. Tina married John Hollingsworth and had two sons, John William and Charles Grady. She has four grandchildren. Tina now lives in Seattle.

In another of Tina's stories in *Elgin, Etc.,* she reminisces about her grandmother Carlson, her Aunt Hulda Lundgren (nee Johnson) and the Swedish community in Elgin. She mentions visiting Sweden as an adult and finding that some Swedes were grateful for those who emigrated in the late 1800s, because it kept the remaining ones from starving.

The visit to Sweden made Tina realize just how very Swedish was her childhood home. Elgin still celebrates Mid-Summer's Day, a Swedish holiday marking the return of long days after the short days of winter. In Texas, the day includes a barbecue. Tina's mother Helen refused to attend the celebration the year she turned ninety. It was the custom to award a fancy cane to the oldest person there. Helen did not want the cane, a visible symbol of being old.

Mama never liked her cousin Helen, and was not very nice to Helen's daughter-in-law Beth, when Beth was trying to collect family history. I never understood all the reasons for the antipathy between the two women. Mama told me in a letter that Helen had called wanting family information. In that letter, Mama implied that she had not been polite to Helen.

Then some time later, Beth Boettcher wrote to her. Mama said that she tried to be friendly to Beth, although Beth might feel differently.

Mama also said in her letter to me that Helen had married two wealthy men and never let the rest of the family forget that she was rich. Mama always felt sensitive about being poor. She never got over the loss of her mother's money in the Depression. I understand from Helen's relatives that Helen was difficult to get along with. So was my Mama, at least with some people!

Arvie was married and divorced three or four times but never had children. His first wife was a Swedish cousin of the neighbor, Betty Lundgren. He was a boxer and farmer in Elgin, and served in the Army during WW II. Swede told me that Arvie had 56 professional boxing matches. Arvie died in 2000, at age 88. He loved horses, and there is one on his gravestone.

Arvie in 1946

Roland (also called "Big Swede") moved to Austin as a young man, and worked on dam projects, then for a time ran a Humble gas station in Austin. He married Martha Mazoch, his sister Helen's college room mate, lived for a while on the Johnson family farm in Elgin, and then moved to El Campo. Big Swede also loved boxing, and helped train a Golden Glove Champion. He died in 1997 at age 79, and was buried in El Campo.

Roland and Martha had one child, Roland (also called Swede), who is a semi-retired lawyer in Victoria, Texas. Swede and his wife Sally Douglas have one daughter, Jenny. They own a part of what was the Johnson family farm, adjacent to the old Carlson farm, which is now owned by the Lundgrens.

Sally told me this story. When Swede and Sally were living on the Johnson farm, Sally took their cat to the vet. The cat had some procedure done, and came home still affected by anesthetic. Swede saw the cat stumbling around and immediately thought she had become rabid. He shot and killed her as a result. The cat story came up in casual conversation, and apparently has been often repeated. I think Sally is still irritated about it.

However, Swede's paranoia about rabies is understandable. His father Roland (Big Swede) was attacked by a dog (possibly rabid) when he was young, and the bites were cauterized to prevent rabies. That was the only preventive available at the time, and was commonly done until the middle of the 20th century, when rabies vaccines were more widely available. Roland was left with a lot of scarring on his back, but fortunately did not develop rabies.

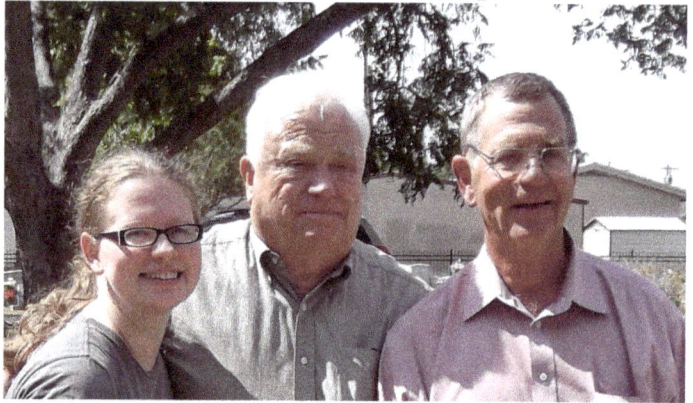

Jenny Carlson (Swede's daughter), Charles Boettcher (Helen's son) and Swede Carlson (Roland's son) in 2012.

Arvid (left) and his brother Richard, in Elgin, late 1920s.

Jennie Augusta Carlson, Carl August's fourth child, never married. She stayed home and helped care for her parents and grandparents (the Persons) and then took care of the household for her brothers Verner and Richard when they were farming in Bishop. She died of cancer in 1923 at age 42.

Jennie as a young woman

Mama told me Jennie's cancer was caused by radium treatments for severe acne as a teenager, and that the cancer started on her face. Her death certificate lists "carcinoma of right shoulder" as the cause of death, so it might have started there instead of her face. I have a photograph of her as a young woman, and one after the cancer started. According to Mama, she would not allow a frontal photograph after the cancer was visible. She wore a gauze mask to cover the tumor on her face.

The use of radium to treat all kinds of ailments was fairly common in the early 1900s. Eventually it was discovered that radium caused cancer, sometimes as long as forty years after exposure. By the 1920s radium was generally recognized as dangerous. But before then, radium was available commercially in water, face powder, suppositories, soap, chocolate, condoms, toothpaste, and lotions. Jennie likely was treated with radium mixed into glycerin or lanolin, and applied to the skin.

Jennie, after the cancer had
started on her face.

Nobody alive remembers Jennie now. I wish I knew
something about her personality and interests.

Ellen Matilda Carlson was the fifth Carlson child. She was
born in 1882. Ellen had rheumatic fever when she was fourteen. This
condition is caused by a bacterial infection (like strep throat) that
damages the heart.

When she died at 81, her cause of death was given as "chronic
rheumatic heart disease, complicated by cerebral arteriosclerosis."
It is amazing that the heart condition did not trouble her unduly
during her long life. But without it, maybe she could have lived into
her nineties, as did her sister Annie.

Ellen as a young woman

Ellen married a Swedish/American plumber, Carl Blomquist, in 1906. He died of flu in January of 1919, toward the end of the Spanish flu epidemic. He was only 36 years old. They had five children:

Verno 1911-1999
Leverne 1915-2002
Chester 1909-1980
Frances Mathilda (Simon) 1907-1984
Anna Genevieve (Pugh) 1918 –

Mama talked about the great flu epidemic, which started the year she was born. Her mother told stories about how terrible it was. She said that in the Swedish/American community, neighbors, sisters and female cousins pitched in to take care of flu patients and their children. But of course the caregivers sometimes got the flu and were either incapacitated or killed. There were weeks when several people in the same family were buried.

In early September, 1918, the *Austin Statesman* newspaper reported that the Spanish flu was really no worse than any other type of flu. There were only a few known cases in Austin at the time. By late October, the numbers of sick exceeded 2,000 and the city closed public schools, the university, pool halls, and churches. They remained closed till January. The epidemic died down a bit and returned the following fall. Texas was not alone in being seriously affected by the Spanish flu. More than 25% of Americans got sick during the pandemic, and almost 700,000 died.

Ellen never remarried. She managed to raise her five children alone, although by 1920 her sister Annie was living with her. Ellen ran boarding houses for University of Texas students, within a few blocks of the campus. At that time students could live only in university-approved housing, and there was a shortage of dorms and approved housing, so she always had renters.

The first of Ellen's boarding houses that I could find was at 303 East 11th Street. The census for 1920 lists Ellen, all her children, and some boarders. They were probably in the house on East 11$^{th}$ St, but I cannot confirm that. Annie's profession is "Nurse, private family."

The 1930 census shows Ellen living with her children Verno, Leverne, and Jennie (Genevieve), and ten boarders. Most of them were young men in their early twenties, born in Texas, but a few were in their thirties, and one was a forty-five year old from Sweden. At that time the City Directory has her at the 11$^{th}$ St. house.

The Blomquists and Annie lived at East 11th St. from sometime before 1930 to about 1936 or 37. Then she purchased another house at 2205 Rio Grande Street. It was called "Blomquist Swedes House." Mrs. Hardin, an across-the-street neighbor, ran a boarding house for female students. Sue told me that Ellen tried for a while to rent to college girls but found them to be too rude, rowdy and badly behaved. She thought that young men could be managed better. Ellen was a tall woman, with big bones. I imagine she could be fairly intimidating if necessary.

Mrs. Hardin's business was passed on to her children, who bought up nearby property and added on to existing buildings. The Hardin family bought Ellen's house on Rio Grande in the 1940s and bricked the exterior, then later enlarged the building. Today "Hardin House" is actually several buildings, including what was once Ellen's house at 2205. That enlarged and bricked building is now addressed as 2207 Rio Grande, and called the "Red House" because of its red-brick facade. The Hardins are still renting to UT women students.

One of Ellen's boarding houses, probably the one on Rio Grande Street

In 1940 Ellen was in the Rio Grande St. house. Of her kids, only Genevieve was still living at home. Genevieve was 21, and a student at U. T. at the time. Annie is not listed in the household. She might have been away delivering a baby, but as far as I know, during that period the two sisters still lived together.

Mama and her two older children, Carl and Sue, visited Ellen and Annie several times in the 1940s at the Rio Grande St. address. My sister Sue always wondered how the two plump sisters could manage in the small bedroom they shared. All the other bedrooms were rented out.

Genevieve from UT yearbook

Mama was particularly fond of Ellen's daughter Genevieve. I never met any of Ellen's children, but in the 7th grade I was the happy recipient of some outgrown clothing from one of Ellen's grand daughters who was a bit older. I am pretty sure she was Genevieve's daughter. It was a bit odd to get boxes in the mail with exquisitely made dresses from a cousin I never met.

I have not been able to locate Genevieve via the Internet, and am not sure whether she is still alive. Ellen's other children have all passed away.

Ellen's picture from
newspaper obituary

After the Rio Grande house was sold, Ellen bought another at 2309 San Antonio Street She was there at least until 1958. Most of the houses in that block are gone now, replaced with office buildings and churches.

When Sue was looking for a wedding gown in 1958, one of Ellen's grandchildren (Verno's daughter) took Sue shopping in Austin. The two young women were about the same age. Verno was the accounts manager at a very nice department store in Austin. He was also part owner of a high end men's clothing store in Austin, called Merritt Schaefer and Brown. It was the custom at the time for upper level department store managers and owners to give and get discounts at each other's stores. The Blomquists were accustomed to getting a knocked-down price when they shopped at the better stores. Sue's cousin made sure she got the Blomquist family discount and paid only $62.00 for her size 11 gown. This was a time when Sue's teaching salary was $3300 a year, so even that reduced price was a lot of money. I wore the same gown when I married in 1967, so the dress ended up being truly a bargain. Neither Sue nor I could possibly fit into that gown now!

Ellen and her husband Carl are both buried in the Palm Valley Lutheran Church Cemetery.

The photograph below shows the front steps of Ellen's boarding house. The picture was taken circa 1921. I assume this was the 11th St house. In the middle is her daughter Frances, and on the lower steps are Ellen (left) and Annie. They are making spring flower arrangements for the house.

August Richard Carlson, the sixth child, was born in 1885. Richard was only four years old when the family moved to America. For many years he lived with his siblings and farmed, and married later in life. Of all the Carlsons, Richard was the one who most closely resembled my grandfather Oscar.

Richard registered for the draft in WW I, and was described as tall, with gray eyes and red hair. He had a large, clear handwriting, and he almost did not get his entire name on the card.

Both Verner and Richard married in 1924. By the time the two brothers married, their sister Nina had been long dead, and sister Ellen was a widow living in Austin. Sister Jennie died in 1923. Sister Annie was living with Ellen to help take care of Ellen's kids as well as maintain her midwifery practice. So all the Carlson sisters were moved away or passed away. I wonder if that contributed to the brothers' decisions to marry. Marriage was sometimes a less romantic and more practical arrangement in those days. A single man had a hard time managing all the work required on a farm, at the same time keeping up with the cooking, cleaning and laundry.

Richard married Iona Lohman when he was 34, and she was 15. Charles Carlson, Richard's youngest son, told me that Iona was "matched" with Richard. I think this means it was an arranged marriage, which was not uncommon at the time. Some members of the family, including my grandfather Oscar, were slightly scandalized by the age difference. On top of that, Richard's wife was not a Swede! According to Mama, it was a strong marriage.

Mama was very fond of Richard and Iona, and my sister Sue remembers his Chihuahuas, Chico and Zapata, who had been taught to "sing" when Richard played his harmonica. I met Richard and Iona once, when I was in elementary school. Mama drove my grandfather Oscar and me to Austin for a visit. I did not meet the boys, but did see their photos on the wall. I remember the adults all drank cups of strong coffee, and I got to taste some of Mama's, with canned milk and sugar. I had no idea then that I would meet Iona's youngest boy when we were both in our sixties.

Iona's family was important in early Texas history. Her grandfather, John Henry Lohmann, was a German immigrant who came to the area near Austin, Texas in 1842. At some point his name spelling changed, and the last "n" was dropped.

John named his first property "Ridgetop." Today that land is the site of the University of Texas. The Lohmans set up the area's first dairy farm, and supplied all of the small, new settlement of Austin with milk. Sixteen years later, John Henry moved to a homestead along the Colorado River about 17 miles northeast of Austin. At one point the river was shallow, coming up only as high as a horse's belly. This area became well used by neighbors who needed to cross the river to get their grain milled, or to visit friends and relatives. It was known as "Lohman's Crossing." The entire area was covered in water in the 1940s, when the state built a reservoir, Lake Travis.

In 1923, when Iona was fifteen, the Lohmans moved to Bishop, Texas. Richard was farming with Verner in Bishop at the time. He and Iona married and farmed cotton on land bordering the famous King Ranch. Their first boy, Richard, was born on their farm in 1928. In 1931 they moved to Elgin, where they worked as tenant farmers.

During the late 1920s, when Richard and Iona were farming near the King Ranch, my own father, Gorman Craven, was helping his parents and brothers survive by illegally hunting rabbits and quail on the King Ranch. This is an interesting connection, but since the King Ranch covered parts of four counties, the area where Papa was hunting and the Carlson farm were probably not very close.

When WW II began, Iona got a job as a military chauffeur at Camp Swift, which was close to Elgin. Camp Swift was built at the start of the war as a military training base. The Camp, with 50,000 men, was a huge (but temporary) boost to Elgin's economy. Locals worked as clerks, carpenters, electricians, phone operators, etc. on base, and the local businesses grew to meet the needs of servicemen. Stores, cafes, and gas stations all benefitted. With the end of the war, the Camp was dismantled, but even then it continued to be useful. Many of the buildings and barracks were moved to Elgin, and became homes, churches, and schools.

When the war ended, Richard and Iona moved to Austin, and in 1947 their second son, Charles, was born. Iona worked for the University of Texas Book Printing Division and Richard was a salesman in a lumberyard. Richard never drove a car or truck, and Iona did all the family driving.

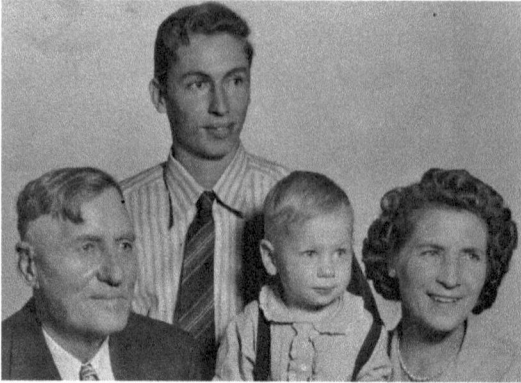

Richard and Iona with sons Richard and Charles, 1948. This was the photo from the Christmas card they sent to Oscar.

Richard, like his brothers Arvid and Oscar, was an alcoholic. He had a stroke in 1963, and this event precipitated a change. He quit drinking and started attending church. He became, in his son Charles' words, "very kind and sober." Charles also told me "the last 10 years of his life were total bliss." Until Richard quit drinking, Iona was the glue that held the family together.

It appears that Richard had several of the common Carlson characteristics: he was a decent man, had some musical talent, loved his family, was a hard worker, and enjoyed animals.

After a decade of sobriety, Richard passed away from renal failure. Iona remarried after Richard died. She and her second husband, Bill Fetner, had three years together before he died of cancer. She was a wonderful singer, and entertained the residents in her nursing home with country songs and hymns.

# Richard's Children

Richard and Iona's oldest son, Richard William Carlson (1928-2014) married Wanda Hollingsworth (b 1931) and had five children: Linda (b 1947), Sterling (b 1950), Don (b 1951), Michael (b 1954) and John (b 1956).

Charles August Carlson, their second son (b 1947), married Kathy Hardin (b 1946) and had two sons: Grady (b 1973) and Andrew (b 1976).

August Richard's sons were born nineteen years apart, so his grandchildren were close in age to his younger son. Charles is the only child of the original Carlson immigrant siblings still alive, since he was born so late in his father's life. Richard was 62 when Charles was born. Charles has been a valuable source of information about the Carlsons.

Charles posted on genforum.com in 2007, saying he was the son of August Richard Carlson, and was looking for family information. I sent him a letter Jan 2, 2013, and he called me back. Charles is a retired educator and a professional photographer. Sue, Beth and I met him in August of 2013 when we went to a convention in San Antonio.

We planned to meet Charles and his wife Kathy in a restaurant near our hotel on the San Antonio River Walk, a beautifully landscaped area by the river, with hotels, shops and restaurants on both sides. We got lost and ended up on the wrong side of the river. I could see our target restaurant across the water, and outside was a tall, handsome white haired man who strongly resembled my brothers. I took a chance and called out, "Charles Carlson!" He waved back. I told him we were lost, and he said to wait. He came across the river, guided us back, and we had a very pleasant lunch with him and his wife Kathy.

Beth, Sue and I were all struck by how much he looked like our brothers. Even his hands resemble theirs. I found out later that his hair had been red before it turned white.

Charles told us he had no knowledge of his dad serving in WWI. We may never know who are in the photo of two men in their WWI uniforms.

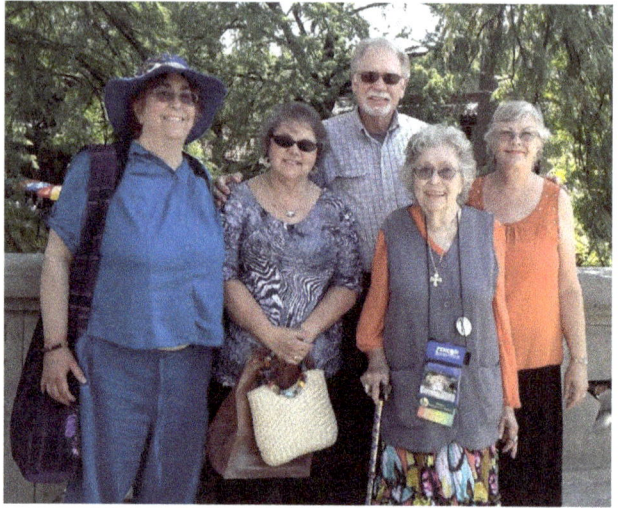

Charles sent me this picture, which he titled "Swedes on the River Walk." From left are: Beth King, Kathy Carlson, Charles Carlson, Susan King, and Gail Fail. August, 2012

Oscar Ivar Carlson was my grandfather, Carl August's sixth child. He was born in 1890, in Round Rock, Texas. Matilda had malaria while she was pregnant with Oscar, and gave birth early. Malaria was fairly common in Texas at the time, and was treated with quinine. It was believed that quinine could cause miscarriage, so as soon as she knew she was expecting, Matilda quit taking the quinine. She was very ill during and after the birth, until the quinine stabilized her again.

Oscar weighed just over 2 pounds at birth and was not expected to live. Matilda was unable to produce enough milk to feed Oscar, because of the early birth and lingering weakness from her illness. In spite of being premature, Oscar had a full head of red hair and an ear-piercing yell.

Carl August had learned in veterinary school that donkey milk was the richest of any domestic animal. He bought a donkey in foal, to get milk for Oscar. It was probably Carl August's veterinary experience that kept Oscar alive. He treated him like any other tiny premature mammal by keeping him warm and feeding him frequently all the family members were involved in helping care for him.

Oscar was only about a foot long at birth. His first bed was a shoebox, and his first diapers were his father's and brothers' handkerchiefs. The older siblings all took turns carrying him around to keep him warm. When he had to be laid down, they placed heated sand bags around the shoebox. Donkey milk and lots of love must have done the trick, because he survived. He was so little that at first he could not suck a standard baby bottle nipple. The family fed him with boiled cotton rags soaked in milk. In modern times, a baby like Oscar would be kept in a NICU.

Starting in 1901, Oscar attended the Lund elementary school. His teacher, Miss Dovie Bradshaw, gave out souvenir cards with her photograph. Oscar must have liked her a lot, because he saved this card for over sixty years. When he was in Miss Bradshaw's class, he would have been 11 years old. Mama told me that he was in a Swedish school before they moved to Lund, and that he did not speak much English until he attended the Lund school.

Miss Bradshaw was unmarried at the time she taught in Lund. She later married, had six children, and outlived Oscar by a few years.

Cards like this one were customary in the early 1900s, and were made for all kinds of purposes. Some businessmen made photograph cards to give out to customers.

This school year (1901-02) was Oscar's first at the Lund school.

The Engblom and Carlson families farmed in Lund and attended the same church, so my grandparents Ella Engblom and Oscar Carlson knew each other while growing up. They were in the same confirmation class in 1904. Oscar was fourteen years old when he was confirmed. Ella was fifteen. I have a small card with the names of everyone in the class. Oscar's and Ella's names are at the bottom. The pastor was J. A. Stamline. I am not sure who wrote the card, but I suspect it was Oscar. He had a distinctive way of writing the "C" in Carlson, and his name on that list closely matches the signature on his WW I draft card.

List of members in Oscar's and Ella's confirmation class.

Oscar and Ella before their marriage.

Oscar and Ella married in 1917. By the time they married, Oscar had long since finished his AA degree in music and business from Trinity Lutheran College in Round Rock. Ella studied Home Economics, but I am not sure whether she actually completed a degree.

After graduation, Oscar worked as a bank clerk in Kenedy, Texas. Ella lived at home with her parents. I am not sure what took them so long to get together. When they married, she was 28 and he was 27. In 1918, they had their only child, Charlotte Rosebell Carlson, my mother.

According to Mama, Ella was considered firmly on the shelf and an old maid before she married. She was even considered a bit old to be having a baby! But Texas Swedish women were in a unique position at that time. There were more young men than women in the Swedish community, so girls could afford to be picky. There was no strong financial pressure to get kids out of the house, as everyone had enough to eat. Many women postponed marriage, or, like Aunt Annie and Aunt Jennie, chose not to marry at all.

Ella (right) and a friend, outside the boarding house where she lived while a college student

Oscar graduated in 1909 from Trinity Lutheran College in Round Rock. He was nineteen years old. There were a total of six graduates that year.

Oscar's college graduating class. He is seated, on the right.

The college offered two-year degrees (the modern equivalent would be an Associate of Arts or Sciences). The institution lasted only 23 years, from 1906 to 1929. For those classes that allowed both men and women students, the women sat separately and were concealed behind a screen.

Trinity Lutheran College

The school finally closed due to lack of students and not enough funding. It was sold to the Lutheran Aid and Orphan Society, to be used for taking care of orphans and the elderly. Most of the college buildings, in bad repair, were torn down in the 1930s, and new buildings put up. One part of the original campus became an assisted living facility for elderly Lutherans, where Oscar's sister Annie spent her last years. The only school structure remaining now is an old stone bath-house.

The first college president was the well-known Dr. J. A. Stamline, the same Lutheran minister who helped found the church that Ella and Oscar attended in Lund. He is the minister who confirmed Oscar and Ella in 1904, and married them in 1917. Their ceremony was held at the Round Rock Lutheran Church. Stamline came to Austin in 1882, and worked as a pastor in Austin and New Sweden. By the time Oscar and Ella married, Dr. Stamline was retired. They persuaded him to perform their marriage ceremony anyway.

Dr. J. A. Stamline

*Swedes in Texas, 1918* said this about Oscar:
OSCAR IVAR CARLSON, Kenedy, an assistant cashier at the First State Bank and Trust Co. in the city. He was born in 1890 in Round Rock, Texas, the son of C.A. Carlson, a veterinary who died in Bishop, Texas, but he had lived in Lund, Travis County, for a long time. Oscar graduated from Trinity College Business School in 1909. He is also a well-trained musician. He serves as organist in the Episcopal Church in Kenedy. His wife, Ella born Engblom, is daughter of Andrew Engblom in Lund. Ella was born in Austin, Texas, in 1890. She also was a student at Trinity College. They married in 1917.

Oscar's and Ella's church wedding certificate, signed by J. A. Stamline.

The room where Ella lived while in college

Ella's Home Economics classes would have included such subjects as sanitary housekeeping and cooking, proper diet, textiles and sewing, care of children, and household economics.

Mama told me that Ella was a fastidious and well-organized housekeeper. She could get up at night, in total darkness, and put her hand on anything she needed in the house. Things were always returned to their proper location after being used. This was certainly not the case in Mama's house!

Ella kept a few chickens and also a couple of goats, since Mama could not tolerate cow's milk. She was an excellent seamstress, and made almost all of her and Mama's clothing, including underwear and hats. Ella's pedal Singer sewing machine, which she got for her sixteenth birthday, was still functional in 1968, when I used it to sew baby blankets and little shirts for my own son.

Oscar was the only one of Carl August's children to get a college degree. This achievement was apparently so significant that over the years, it was inflated in family history to the point that Swede Carlson believed Oscar had a master's degree in Music and taught at the University of Texas in Austin. Actually, he worked as a bookkeeper, and periodically taught music to children, part time. He must have had more patience with these children than he did with his own grandchildren, because all of us refused more lessons after only a few. Any piano talent we may have had was quickly squelched.

When Oscar lived in Corpus Christi in the 1940s, he taught children with varying disabilities. He often spoke about a child with Down's syndrome who learned to play several simple songs. He was very proud of that. I always thought it was an interesting contradiction that he had so little patience with his own relatives. Mama could not learn from him either!

As a young man, he could play almost anything: percussion instruments, woodwinds, stringed instruments, organ and piano. He lost the ability to play any instrument but piano when he injured his right hand in the late 1940s. He was banging on a window that had got stuck, and the glass shattered, cutting his hand in several places. The tendons were cut, and his fingers were permanently closed in a claw shape. He exercised his hand diligently to regain even a little flexibility, and could manage to play piano by hitting the keys with his knuckles. Other instruments were impossible. He learned to write with his left hand, and developed a beautiful old-fashioned style of handwriting. I never heard him complain about the disability or the pain he must have suffered.

Before his hand injury, Oscar practiced calligraphy. He was so skilled that he was asked to handwrite wedding invitations, birth announcements and other papers. Engraving such things cost a lot more money, and his hand-written work was just as beautiful. This talent helped bring in a little money.

After they married, Oscar and Ella rented a house in Kenedy, Texas, a small town south of Austin. He got a paying job as organist in the Episcopal Church there. Oscar, like the rest of his and Ella's family, was raised as a Lutheran. I had always thought he was a life-long Lutheran, although I did not ever see him attend church. My sister Sue told me that when Oscar and Ella started attending the Episcopal Church, it caused a great flap in the family. Some of Ella's relatives came to Oscar's and Ella's home in Kenedy and tried to convince the couple to go back to the true church. Sue remembers being told by Mama that Charlotte Engblom, Ella's mother, said she would rather see her daughter dead and in her grave than in a different church. I wonder how much of the change in churches was due to the fact that the Episcopals paid Oscar to play!

Sue told me that when they moved to Corpus Christi, Ella and Oscar attended a Presbyterian Church. Mama liked the new church, because the Presbyterian pastor gave sermons that were less scary than in the Lutheran Church. She said the Lutherans had too many "thou shalt nots" instead of "thou shalls." The Presbyterian pastor had even quoted how many times each phrase was used in the Bible, and he said that God had more "shalls" than "shall nots."

Oscar's and Ella's first house, in Kenedy, Texas

100

In 1917, the year he married, Oscar was working at First State Bank and Trust, Kenedy, Texas as an assistant cashier. Below is photo of him with his co-workers, all in spiffy straw hats. Oscar has an X on his shirt.

During the late 1800s and early 1900s the railroad system was being built in Texas. Kenedy is a small town that was founded in 1886. The town was named after Mifflen Kenedy, who was one of the railroad barons building in that area during the 1880s. It was first called Kenedy Junction, because the railroad formed a Y at Kenedy, with one branch going to Corpus Christi and the other to Houston. Local agriculture focused on cotton and flax. Today, Kenedy calls itself the "Flax Capital of Texas." The railroad was instrumental in helping Kenedy farmers get crops to market, and in taking people across the state to other cities.

The Masons (Independent Order of Odd Fellows) had a group in Kenedy, and Oscar became a member. It might have been an expected thing for a young man to do, if he wanted to advance in his job and in local society. He continued his membership after he moved away from Kenedy. He was attending a Mason's meeting in Corpus Christi when he injured his hand on the stuck window.

Just before he married, Oscar registered for the draft. The signature he wrote on his draft card is beautiful, but does not look like the signature I remember, from after he injured his right hand. He is described as tall, with a slender build, brown eyes and red hair. The eye color is an error. He had blue eyes.

When Mama was a small child, Oscar's parents were both dead, but Ella's were still alive and living in Austin. Mama had many happy memories of visiting Anders and Lotten Engblom. She often stayed with them several days at a time. Grandma Engblom told her stories of Norse mythology and of her own childhood in Sweden. Mama wrote a very sweet story about chasing rainbows in her grandparents' yard on a day when the weather conditions were perfect for seeing several partial rainbows.

Ella, Rosebell and Oscar in 1924

Oscar, Ella, Bell, Iona and Richard, in 1928

The 1929 stock market crash severely hurt the First State Bank and Trust, and Oscar lost his job. The Bank and Trust was merged with Nichols National Bank under the name First Nichols National Bank in 1933. Amazingly, that bank is still in business.

With the crash, Oscar and Ella lost their house, and Ella lost the money she inherited from her father. All of it was in bank accounts. I am not sure how much money there was, but the family had lived a very comfortable lifestyle. I cannot imagine that Oscar's bookkeeping job was lucrative enough to support them in style. They had a new house, very nice furniture with Oriental rugs, and a car. Mama had crooked teeth as a young child, and got braces on them so her adult teeth would come in properly. This was an unusual dental practice at the time, except for those with enough money. Mama told my brother Carl that Ella had about a million dollars before the Depression. I think the amount was an exaggeration, given my mother's tendency to stretch the truth.

Rosebell at age 10, wearing a new dress Ella sewed for her

Ella was a very modern woman. She had learned in college about the Germ Theory, and used Lysol disinfectant to prevent spreading microbes. Mama explained the germ theory to me when I was in elementary school. She had learned it from her mother, and she complained that my Craven grandmother did not believe it. This was a slur on Grandma Stella, who kept a neat looking but not very sanitary home.

Ella thought that young girls should have their own bodies and the biology of reproduction explained to them. Her own mother, Lotten, did not explain any of this to Ella, and when she began to menstruate at about age sixteen, she thought she was dying. Her clothing was stained, and she was afraid of getting in trouble for ruining her skirt and drawers. She took her clothing to a stream and washed the items, then sat in the cold water in hopes that the bleeding would stop. She made herself so ill that Lotten called a doctor. He explained what had happened to her. Ella made herself a promise that she would not allow her own daughter to go though such a traumatic experience.

In 1930 Oscar, Ella and twelve-year-old Bell were living in Corpus Christi. Oscar was working as the manager of the Seguin Milling and Flour Company in Corpus. Ella died in April 1930 of kidney disease and Oscar lost his job at the mill in July. By that time the Great Depression had set in all over the country.

Mama told us many times that her mother died of pneumonia. According to her story, Ella was sick for a couple of months, and was in the hospital several times. She got progressively worse, and then seemed to rally. The doctor warned Oscar that she was still critically ill, in spite of seeming to feel better for a few hours. She died quietly at home.

Mama was paranoid about pneumonia her entire life. When she was in her seventies and had several bouts with pneumonia herself, she expected each time that it would kill her, as it did her mother. But Ella's death certificate states she died of chronic nephritis, and there is no mention of pneumonia.

Nephritis is a kidney disease. It can be caused by a strepto-coccal infection or an allergic reaction to medication, but most commonly it is due to an autoimmune disease. Somehow, Mama got the impression that it was a lung problem that killed her mother. Shortness of breath is a common symptom of nephritis, so that might explain her confusion. I imagine that she and Oscar did not do much discussion about the details of Ella's death in the following years. Apparently he fell into a bottle not long after the funeral and stayed there for the next three decades. He never completely dried out until his final illness, although his binge drinking slowed down in the 1950s.

Oscar worked various jobs after Ella's death: he was a longshoreman, gardener, and a piano teacher, till his clothes got too shabby to enter the homes of the relatively wealthy people who hired him to teach their kids. He finally got a full time job at the Naval Base in Corpus Christi, in the receiving department. Some of the things he "received" were weapons that were to be used to protect the president. When he was in his last illness, and confused about where and when he was, he told Mom, "You must not tell anyone this. We must protect the president. He's crippled." I heard this last from my brother Jerry. Of course, Oscar was referring to President Roosevelt, who was in office from 1933 till 1945.

During the Depression, Oscar and Bell lived for a few years in a cheap rented house in a Mexican barrio in Corpus Christi. Oscar figured that maybe his beautiful teenaged daughter would be safer with a bunch of family-oriented Mexican Catholics than in the poorer white neighborhoods. The house they rented had dirt floors, a wood stove, and a cold water tap in the back yard. They put Ella's oriental rugs on the dirt floor. Most of Ella's furniture and other possessions had been sold. Her treadle sewing machine went to a relative, although Mama got it back for a while in the late 1960s.

This must have been a really stressful time for Bell and Oscar. It became her job to get Oscar up and dressed for work, and drag him home from bars at night. She threw out any alcohol she found in the house.

Bell's High school graduation picture, 1935

During the Depression when Oscar was working as a gardener, he would walk home each afternoon and get threatened by an aggressive dog along the way. The animal would rush out of its yard, bark, growl and snarl. Then one day the dog actually bit him on the leg. Oscar was so enraged by this that he stabbed the dog several times with a pair of sharp pruning shears. The dog was not fatally injured, but after that he left Oscar alone. This story astonished me the first time I heard it. I never saw him show anyone any violence, and he was especially gentle with animals and kids. The worst I ever experienced was when he yelled at me if I crossed the street without his holding my hand, and once he used a "switch" (a long blade of grass) on my legs. Of course, I never bit him on the leg, either.

In 1935 my mother married Gorman Craven. In the early years of their marriage, they moved around Texas and Arkansas, following the construction work. My father was a plumber. Their marriage was rocky almost from the start, and for a while (before I was born) they were separated. Papa took a job in Port Aransas, Texas and Mama lived in Corpus Christi with Oscar. Frances Tipton Carlson's daughter Marie got Mama a job at the telephone company. Oscar was working at the naval base. Mama and Oscar together bought a little house on Cloyd St.

The house had only two bedrooms. Sue slept on the couch in the living room and Oscar shared a room with the boys. Papa finally persuaded Mama to take him back. At first he was on the couch at night and Sue slept with Mama. But after a while, Sue was back on the couch and Papa was back in Mama's bed. The marriage survived for another thirty years. Their relationship was generally dysfunctional but they did have periods of relative peace.

My parents took their three children to Venezuela in the late forties and returned five years later with their last child. Oscar married again just before the family went to Venezuela. He and his second wife Ann ran a small grocery and liquor store in Corpus Christi. While the family was out of the country, Ann, also an alcoholic, died of liver failure.

Oscar in 1949, in Corpus Christi

Ann made Sue a traveling suit for the family's trip to Venezuela. Sue was almost done with 6$^{th}$ grade, and the outfit was very grown up. Sue liked Ann, but Mama never cared for her. She disapproved of anyone who encouraged her Daddy's drinking.

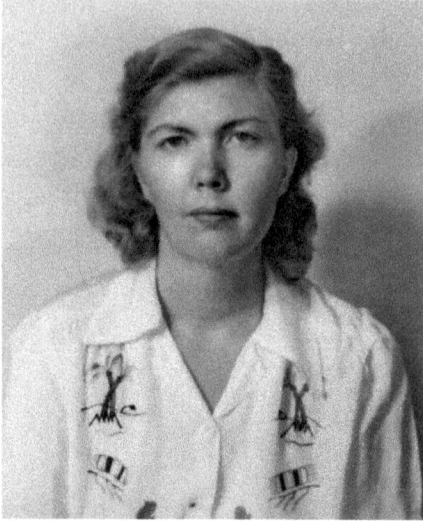

Bell, just before going to Venezuela.

The five-year stay in Venezuela was an adventure for Papa and the boys. Sue was not too thrilled with it because she was not allowed to leave the house much. The boys, considered less likely to be molested or kidnapped, had a wonderful time. Mama enjoyed parts of it, but I think it was extremely difficult for her as well. She worried (with cause) about tropical diseases, snakes, and other biting critters. She was sure she had leprosy at one time, but it turned out to be a reaction to Papa's foot fungus medicine, which she got on her fingers whenever she applied it to his toes. After a botfly laid an egg in Jerry's scalp, the doctor removed a half-inch larva. It was more distressing to Mama than to Jerry, who thought it was cool. We all got intestinal worms and were successfully treated. After that we got regular doses of worm medicine. A huge centipede in Mama's closet bit her and dug its poisoned feet into her arm, leaving her with a neat row of boils. All this may have toughened our mother a bit, because she never showed any real fear of anything that I remember, other than an occasional encounter with a spider.

When the family returned to Texas in the early 1950s they had another child: me. My Craven cousins worried that I might be brown skinned because I was born in the tropics, but I was as fair skinned and blonde haired as all the rest of Mama's children. We lived for a while with relatives, including a short stay with Oscar in Corpus Christi. My father got a plumbing job in Port Arthur and when we moved there, Oscar retired and came along. He lived with my parents until he died in 1967.

The children in my family called Oscar "Daddy Pop." This name came about because our mother called him "Daddy," but our father, who knew Oscar before he met our mother, called him "Pop," a nickname that had been bestowed upon him by the men working at the Naval Base. The kids just combined both names.

After we moved to Port Arthur, Daddy Pop took over responsibility for the kitchen, much of the cooking, and the yard. He was also my primary baby sitter, since both my parents worked and the older kids were in school. I spent more time with him than with any of my other family members, starting when I was about four and a half years old. I loved him unconditionally, although his behavior was sometimes peculiar.

Daddy Pop's small Social Security check was helpful in paying his personal expenses (like cigarettes and whiskey) and sometimes was used for groceries for the family when my parents were broke. He chain-smoked Pall Malls, and every Christmas Mama gave him a couple of cartons. He also drank secretly. I never saw him falling down drunk. His breath had a constant smell of liquor, so he must have been a bit inebriated all the time. I did not recognize the odor until I was grown and smelled whiskey in a bottle for the first time. My parents knew about Daddy Pop's addiction but never talked about it in front of me. As a result, I accepted his smell and his occasional odd behavior. I think they often did not notice his alcohol breath because they were not sitting in his lap, as I was.

I figured out many years later that I was his method for sneaking bottles into the house. We lived in a large, two-story house. Daddy Pop and the kids had bedrooms upstairs, and my parents made the downstairs dining room into their bedroom. I was regularly asked to take small items up and down the stairs, to save somebody else the climb. I frequently carried up small paper bags, of books, cigarettes, snacks and other things for Daddy Pop. The rest of the family never questioned what I was toting, as it was often something for one of them. I left his paper bags where he instructed, either in his bedroom or in mine. He often left them in my closet. Mama periodically came up to "clean" his bedroom, and search for alcohol. She never cleaned my bedroom, or my brothers' bedroom, so his whiskey was pretty safe in my closet.

The secrecy about Oscar's alcoholism was the norm for the time. There was never an attempt to get him into AA or any other treatment program. My mother was embarrassed about his drinking, and she had some difficult times after Ella died and he started drinking heavily. She saw his being alcoholic as a failure to be strong, or a weak moral character. She loved him anyway.

Daddy Pop kept busy with gardening, caring for his parakeet and about a dozen yard cats, working crossword puzzles, and watching out for me. He was a master gardener and could do fancy things like grafting different colors of roses onto the same rootstock. He usually planted a small vegetable garden in the back yard, and every summer we had green beans, tomatoes, squash and peppermint, plus whatever he decided to try that year. He was very interested in nature and was the original stimulus for my interest in biology. He read widely, and in spite of having a somewhat damaged brain from alcohol, tobacco and arteriosclerosis, remembered a lot of what he read. He was the first person to explain a life cycle to me.

Like the rest of his family, Oscar had a sense of humor and liked to tell tall tales. My mother and my brother Jerry inherited that tendency. By the time I was eight or nine I had learned to discount a lot of what Daddy Pop or Jerry told me. Because of that I did not believe Daddy Pop's explanation of a slime mold's life cycle when he told me. I thought it was too outrageous to be true. Later, I had to eat my words.

110

Daddy Pop taught me a lot of things. He showed me how to use a broom properly to sweep the floor. He did not use a fancy metal dustpan for the sweepings. He just dampened the edge of a piece of newspaper and swept the dirt onto it. I was not very good at it for the first few dozen sweepings. But once I mastered the art, he never swept the floors again.

He taught me some other homely things: how to make coffee in the stove top percolator, boil an egg, crack a raw egg without making a mess, cook oatmeal, wash dishes, distinguish weeds from vegetable seedlings, and cross the street safely. He raised his voice at me periodically, but the only time he seemed really mad at me was when I was four. I stole a nickel from his room and crossed the street alone to buy an ice cream. He switched my legs with a bit of grass. It did not really hurt, but I yelled a lot anyway, in case he decided to get serious about it.

Oscar had a life-long problem with his temper. He and Mama would get into terrible arguments over minor things. They would both shout and stomp around. Mama scared me when she got mad, but I was never afraid of Daddy Pop. Looking back, I wonder whether his temper fits happened more frequently when he was drunker.

I never once talked to Daddy Pop about religion, and to this day I am not sure of his core beliefs. My own religious education was eclectic, as my parents had differing and somewhat bizarre ideas. I am not sure of Daddy Pop's political views, either. I do know that he was a fairly conservative man in most things and was strongly in favor of proper dress, decorum and the wearing of hats.

Daddy Pop loved music but disapproved of rock and roll. He especially disliked Elvis Presley. He watched the Beatles with me when they appeared on the Ed Sullivan show, but he was unimpressed.

As he grew older, Daddy Pop developed dementia. He had several small strokes, and his arteries were clogged. Many years of drinking, smoking, and eating a very high fat diet contributed to plaque buildup and loss of elasticity in his arteries. He would forget where he was, or how to get home, even though his memory of things that happened forty years earlier was intact. When I was in high school, his dementia reached a point where it was not safe to leave him alone at home. He wandered away one day and fell, wounding his good hand and getting a lot of dirt and gravel in the abrasion. After that, Mama hired help to make sure he was never alone. Mama worked at the telephone company, and would be home with him in the mornings. Then she went to work and a "housekeeper" would come until I got home from school. I watched him then until Mama got home from work around 10 PM. I was responsible for him all day when school was not in session.

We had several "housekeepers." They actually did some housework. One of them was a great cook and would start dinner before she went home. She taught me a bit about cooking. A couple of them did ironing. But each woman's main job was to make sure Daddy Pop did not wander away from the house or get hurt. Mostly, that meant listening to him talk.

Daddy Pop died in 1967 about four months after I left home for college, from a series of strokes. During his last weeks, I spent some time with him at the hospital and he thought I was his dead wife Ella. He spoke to me so affectionately that it made me realize how much he had loved my grandmother, and what a blow it must have been to lose her.

After he had been in the hospital for almost a month, getting progressively worse, he slipped into unconsciousness. A few days later our family doctor told Mama that she had to let her father go. He said that Oscar was hanging on because Mama was so upset at losing him, and that in spite of being in a coma, Oscar was aware of her distress. She had been spending every possible minute with him, talking and crying, and maybe feeling guilty for all the times she yelled at him. Taking the doctor's advice, she went to Oscar's bedside and told him that it was all right to die, and that she would be fine. In just a few minutes, he was gone.

Richard and Annie were still alive when Oscar died. Richard told Mama that it was a shame Oscar had died so young (he was 77).

The others lasted into their eighth decade, except for Annie, who lived to age 96. Richard said the entire family had expected Oscar to die young since he was born premature and had always been puny. Oscar was small for a Carlson boy, and skinny his entire life.

The last two of Carl August's nine children, Nina and Eric, died young. I remember that Mama told me they were twins born in Sweden, and that Oscar was the only one born in America, but this was wrong. Nina's grave is in the Lund cemetery, and the date of birth on her stone is 1896, so she was born after the Carlsons arrived in Texas. I have never seen a record that she and Erik were twins. Another family tree on Ancestry.com says that Erik was born in Sweden in 1896, and died as an infant. However, this birth date means he must also have been born in America.

Nina died in 1911, at age 15. Mama told me that Nina died of a fever. It could have been any of a number of infectious diseases that are now treatable.

My brother Jerry says that he remembers Mom saying that Oscar, Nina and Erik were all born in the U. S., and that Erik died at age two. I think this is more likely. If Erik did die at two and had been born in 1896, then he would have died before the family moved to Lund. He might be buried in Round Rock but is not included in any cemetery listing for that city or the surrounding communities. There is nobody left now who can remember Nina and Erik directly.

Nina Carlson at about age six.

In her photograph, young Nina is wearing a plumed hat that seems too large for her slender neck. She even has her head tilted, as if the hat is too heavy. The fancy hat was probably rented from the photographer. In Sweden, only the very wealthiest people could afford fancy hats, and most women wore simple home made caps or scarves. After becoming relatively affluent in America, many Swedes had photos taken wearing the biggest, most elaborate hats available. It was a visible symbol of affluence.

The Carlson siblings at a reunion in the early 1960s:
Ellen, Richard, Arvid, Oscar, Annie, and Verner.

Mama was intelligent and beautiful but emotionally unstable. She could get along just fine for many months without a crisis, and then dive into a bout of severe depression or delusional thinking. I have often wondered if she had bipolar disorder. She had some physical health issues that may have contributed to depression, including irritable bowel syndrome and stomach ulcers. But in spite of her emotional and physical problems, she tried hard to be a good mother, and truly loved her kids. She gave us all a fondness of reading, an appreciation of a good story, and a lot of affection.

Mama had many small strokes, or Transient Ischemic Attacks (TIAs). I think she may have started having TIAs in her forties, but in her seventies they became more common. Just after each TIA she would show some signs of it, with difficulty in remembering words, short-term memory loss, or with an interesting hallucination. The hallucinations were colorful, realistic waking dreams in which people she knew were up to no good.

For example, she once hallucinated that my brother-in-law was having an affair with his secretary and was also embezzling from his boss. Mama believed she had seen him on television, being dragged out in handcuffs, shirtless, with his partially clothed secretary behind him. I was never able to convince her this did not occur and in fact could not have occurred. My brother-in-law did not have a secretary or a boss to embezzle from; he managed a fast food restaurant, and was his own boss. Most of her delusions faded with time, and she seemed to forget them. She would have periods of perfect lucidity, when she was pleasant, affectionate, smart, and funny.

Mama never got a college degree. She married Papa immediately after high school graduation and started having babies right off the bat. When I was a teenager, she managed to take a few classes at Lamar University. But it was too difficult to manage college courses, a full time job, a teenager at home, an aging father, and a husband who did not support her desire for education. She always regretted not having attended nursing or medical school when she was young, and she insisted that her own children would get college educations. When she saw I had an interest in biology, she did everything but stand on her head to persuade me to major in medicine, which is what she had wanted to study.

Mama was strongly affected by her mother's premature death, the Great Depression, World War II, and her father's drinking. She had a fairly comfortable retirement, partly because she lived in one of Sue's rental houses in Big Spring, paying only a token rent. But she always felt more secure with some money hidden in the house for emergencies (she did not much trust banks), and a stock of food. When she died, we went through her house and found dozens of packs of dried noodles, canned food and other edibles tucked away in various drawers and closets. She routinely hid money behind electrical switch plates, in a bucket of sand in her hot water heater closet, and in her nightstand. When the planes hit the World Trade Center, she called me and told me to turn on the television and then go withdraw cash from the bank, in case we were at war. She also advised me to stock up on food.

Mama was a strong feminist. She was a union steward at the telephone company, and in 1966 she led the fight to allow telephone operators to wear pants at work. She was working in the Beaumont, Texas, office, and pants suits were all the rage in women's fashions. Bell Telephone still had some outdated rules regarding dress code for operators, which Mama thought was silly, especially since none of the customers ever saw the operators anyway. The company allowed miniskirts, but not slacks, which were actually more modest.

The company's rules said that anyone deemed to be dressed inappropriately had to be sent home to change. The trip home was at company expense if the woman did not have a car of her own. So for about a week, Mama (and all the other women she could persuade to join her) wore pants to work, knowing they would be sent home to change. Bell Telephone got tired of paying for all those round trip taxi rides, especially for women who, like Mama, lived a considerable distance away. Her male supervisor finally told her, "I give up, you win." At the time, I was attending high school, which still did not allow girls on campus to wear pants!

Years later, after she and my father divorced, Mama applied for a switchman position, a traditionally male-only job in the phone company. She put on her union hat to pressure the company into letting her take the training required for the job. She passed all the classes with high marks and got the job in spite of obstacles put up by the trainers. This dramatically increased her salary and assured a comfortable pension when she retired.

Before she got the switchman job, Mama commuted to Beaumont from Vidor, working night shifts as a phone operator. She bought a 22-caliber handgun and put it (loaded) in her glove box. There had been a series of molestations and robberies of night shift workers in downtown Beaumont. One night a group of drunken young men surrounded her car and tried to frighten her at a stop-light. They pushed on the car, rocking it back and forth. She took out her gun and aimed it at the closest one, and they scattered.

My brother Jerry sent me this about our Mama. It is about a time when Jerry and his family were living in Malaysia and Mama came to see them.

"She came to Malaysia for a visit, went shopping in the native mall in Kuala Lumpur, got mugged, her purse stolen, and she shrugged it off. She sat outside my house barefooted, smoked a long skinny cigar, and picked up a bacterial infection in her toe. Hobbled around with me to the Ghenting Highlands gambling resort, played the slots. I stood for a long while off to one side watching her feed the machine and pull the lever all the while with her mouth slightly open and a black cigarette stuck to and hanging from a lower lip, looking like a superannuated gangster moll. She gambled away twenty ringgits in change (eight dollars) and loved the process. I kept orchids all over her room—these were cheaper than mums over there, and she said the orchids made her feel like a queen. So at seventy she went to another third world country for an adventure and enjoyed every minute of it."

In high school, Mama met a girl named Gail Laverne Livingston, whose parents, Jesse Roy and Laura, had a bakery. The two girls became best friends, and Mama worked part time in the Livingston family bakery before she married. In her early thirties, just before my family moved to Venezuela, Gail died of breast cancer. Mama cared for Gail during her final illness. By this time, Mama had three children and had been told she probably could not conceive another.

Just before she died, Gail told Mama that they would be together again, and that she would come back reincarnated as Mama's fourth child. A few years later, when I was born, she named me Gail Laverne. I did not know until I was grown that Mama thought I was the reincarnation of the first Gail. When I arrived at her home in South Texas to care for her after gall bladder surgery, she hugged me and said, "Now it's your turn to take care of me!"

I had fewer disagreements with Mama than did the older kids. I think it was partly because I was so much younger, and she had less energy with me. But I also think that believing me to be her dead friend made a difference in her attitude.

My parents divorced after Daddy Pop died. Both of them remarried. Mama married the widower of an old family friend, Glenn Meek. He died a few years before her, but they lived happily and with much less tension than Mama had with my father.

Glenn was a retired high school teacher. He willed his body to the Lubbock Texas Tech medical school for dissection, saying that it was the last chance he would have to teach a student anything. Mama liked the idea, and did the same thing.

A few years before she died, Mama came to see me in California, and I gave her a tour of the anatomy classroom at the college where I taught. She was very interested in seeing the cadavers used for teaching anatomy to nursing students, and told me then she had decided to will her body for dissection. Her body, like Glenn's, was cremated after being used as a learning tool for the med students. Their ashes are interred near the medical school in Resthaven Memorial Park Cemetery under a stone that reads, "In memory of those that have given of themselves so that others may live in health and happiness."

# Our Grandmother Ella's family: the Engbloms and Westlings

Ella's father was Andrew (Anders) Norgaard Engblom. He was born in 1852, in Vasa, Finland to a Finnish father and a Swedish mother. He died in 1925 at age 73. Anders married Charlotte (Lotten or Lottie) Westling in 1886. She was born in Sweden in 1855 and immigrated to America with her parents and siblings. They eventually settled in central Texas. Anders and Lotten had four children: Ella Johanna Engblom 1889-1930, Frank Theodore Engblom 1891-

1965, and Rudolph Lorentz Engblom 1897-1971. Another boy, whose name I don't know, died as a toddler.

In separate parts of *Swedes in Texas*, Ella's mother's name is given as Lotten Westling, Johanna Charlotta, and Josephine Charlotte.

"Lotten" and "Lottie" are both derivatives of Charlotte. Mama, whose name was Charlotte Rosebell, told me that she was named after her mother's mother. Ella's brothers were called Theodore (pronounced "Thay-der") and Rudolph.

The Engblom children: Rudolph (left, in a dress), Theodore and Ella. Circa 1898. Their ages were 1, 3, and 11.

Here is the history that Mama told us about her maternal grandparents:

Anders Norgaard had a Finnish father and a Swedish mother. He ran away from his home in Finland at age 12, and became a sailor. At some point, he learned carpentry. Anders changed his name to Engblom (a Swedish name meaning "meadow flower") to prevent his Finnish family from finding him.

Anders before coming to America

Mama told me that Anders was a ship captain, but he was actually the first mate on the cargo ship that carried the Westling family to America. He befriended the entire family, and in particular noticed the oldest Westling daughter, but at the time he was married and his Swedish wife was pregnant. His wife gave birth and died while he was at sea. After she died, Anders gave the child (a boy) to his dead wife's family and went to America. In later years he tried to locate his son, even hiring private detectives, but never found him.

Apparently Lotten liked Anders from the beginning, but their relationship on the ship was limited to a few polite conversations. After all, he was a married man. But once Anders' wife died, he decided that he needed a different life style. He felt a lot of guilt about being away from his Swedish wife when she was alive, and being gone when she died in childbirth added to that guilt. He decided to move to America and start a new life. He had some money put away, and his skill as a carpenter would assure employment.

Charlotte (Lotten) Westling, around 1880

Anders wrote to the Westlings where they had settled in Bridgeport, Connecticut, and they assured him that coming to America was a good idea. He was functionally illiterate, so somebody else had to write the letters for him and read the replies.

The Westlings later moved to Texas. Anders followed them there, and proposed to Charlotte. Charlotte's father told Anders that he could not marry Charlotte unless he gave up the sea, and was financially secure. Anders had already decided that he was done with life as a sailor. He worked several years in Galveston and saved his money until he had a large enough nest egg to support his bride. Anders was frugal, and very good at managing money. But it took several years before he was well off enough to convince Lotten's father that he could support a wife. Lotten waited almost five years for him. Their marriage was a real love match, and they were very happy together. Mama thought her grandparents had an ideal marriage.

Lotten and Anders just before their wedding in 1886.

After a few years in Galveston, he moved to Austin, where he helped to build the Capitol building. He took some of his pay in land rather than cash, and eventually settled in Lund to farm cotton.

Anders' father was (according to Mama), a Finnish nobleman. He was the youngest of several sons and married a Swedish girl with no particular political connections. Her father was a timber merchant. They had several children, including Anders, and lived just outside of Vasa in a hunting lodge that belonged to the Finnish grandfather. A "plague" killed Anders' father's older brothers, making him the heir. His family made him leave his Swedish wife, dissolved the marriage, and forced him to remarry, this time to a suitable Finnish noblewoman. This family disruption caused Anders to run away.

This is a great story, but I am not sure how much truth is in it. The nobility part makes me suspicious. But it is true that Anders changed his name, and that he was both a carpenter and a sailor. I had his church hymnal (written in Swedish) until it finally fell apart and turned completely to fragments. On the inside cover, which is all that is left, someone had written his name: Anders Norgaard. The *Norgaard* was scratched out and he had written in *Engblom*. You can just make out the "rg" in Norgaard.

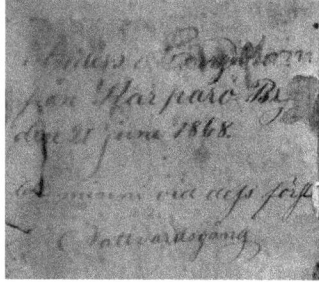

The city where Anders was born is spelled Vasa in Swedish and Vaasa in Finnish. Vasa is a mid sized coastal city in western Finland; it was built by a Swedish king in 1606. It has long been a center for shipping, particularly for the export of pitch and tar, derived from coniferous tree resin and used for water-proofing objects and caulking wooden ships. Since Vasa's founding, at a time when Finland was controlled by Sweden, there have been many Swedish-speaking people in the town. A lot of Finnish/Swedish marriages resulted, including that of Anders' parents.

The year before Anders was born, most of the city burned when someone fell asleep in a barn and dropped a lighted pipe. If Mama's story is true, Anders' family would have been spared the fire because they lived outside of town.

In the 1860s when Anders was a boy, the timber industry in Finland was booming. The tariffs on Finnish wood and wood products were reduced in Great Britain, and the Finnish government ended its firm control of forest cutting. Canals and railroads were being built, and trade with Russia and the rest of Europe opened up. Anders' mother, as the daughter of a timber merchant, was probably well to do.

I am not sure why Anders was so poorly educated. I have often wondered if he had a learning disability. After they married, Lotten patiently taught him to read and write Swedish. Eventually, he learned English and a bit of Spanish. Both Lotten and Anders were strongly in favor of education for their own children. They sent all three to the Lutheran college in Round Rock.

I found an 1881 record of Anders Engblom as a crewmember on the Wearmouth, a British cargo ship that also carried a few passengers between America and England. He is listed there as married, so this was before his first wife died. That same year he quit the sea and came to Texas, where he landed first in Galveston. He immediately went to work as a carpenter and lived in a boarding house. In 1886 he got a job working on the Capitol building in Austin, and he married Lotten. They rented a house on East 18th St, near the area called Swedish Hill. Within a year, they moved to another house on East Avenue, also in the Swedish Hill neighborhood.

Swedish Hill is an area close to downtown that was originally an almost entirely Swedish enclave, starting in the 1870s. There are still some well-maintained historic houses there.

The capitol building was finished in 1888. The next year Anders and his father-in-law Jonas Westling both got land in Lund. (Anders' land was part of his pay for the Capitol work.) The first Engblom baby, my grandmother Ella, was born the same year. By 1894, the year Lotten's mother Joanna died, Anders and Lotten were established cotton farmers in Lund. Jonas moved in with them that same year. He was sixty-six years old.

It was not until the 1870s that commercial window screens were available in the U. S. Anders was so taken with the concept of window screening that he had screens put on all his farmhouse windows. He also added screen doors to the outside *and* the inside doors. Having a screen door on a bedroom seems like overkill to me. Maybe Anders really hated mosquitoes.

Anders must have done well, because in the 1918 book *Swedes in Texas*, he is described as a "well to do farmer." Mama described him as a "self-made millionaire."

Giving up the sea might have saved his life. His ship, the Wearmouth, sank off the coast of Canada within months of his leaving. Only five of the crew of 20 survived.

By the time my mother was born in 1918, Anders and Lotten had retired from farming and were living on Leona St. in Austin, about a mile northeast of the Capitol.

Mama described Anders as handsome, with black eyes, brown hair and a strong, stocky build. He was five feet and four inches tall. His wife Lotten was six feet tall and fair. They both got plumper as they aged, and in the formal photograph I have of them with baby Rosebell, Lotten is seated in a lower chair than he, so the height difference does not show.

Anders and Lotten holding baby Rosebell, 1918.

Below is Anders' signature from the stub of his naturalization papers. He was seventy years old at the time he signed this. His handwriting seems to indicate he was still somewhat uncomfortable with writing.

(Signature of holder)

certificate. No 1723087

According to *Swedes in Texas*, the Swedish Lutheran Bethlehem Congregation in Lund was founded under the leadership of Dr. Stamline, on January 16, 1897, with 19 active members and 20 children. Anders and his family members were among the charter members, and Anders was a trustee.

*Swedes in Texas*, 1918, said this about him:

ANDERS ENGBLOM was born in Vasa, Finland, in 1853. He became a carpenter and then a sailor. In 1880 he came to Galveston, Texas, and is now a well to do farmer in Lund, Travis County, Texas. In 1886 he married Lotten Westling, daughter of inspector Jonas Westling. She was born in Slaka parish, Östergötland, and came to America in 1880. She first lived in Bridgeport, Conn. The Engbloms have three children: Eleonora, Theodore and Rudolph. The family belongs to the Swedish Lutheran Congregation in Lund.

The year of his arrival in this book does not agree with Anders' immigration record, which has it a year later.

Grandmother Lotten in 1926, after Anders died.

Anders and Lotten's sons, Frank Theodore and Rudolph Lorentz, were farmers as young men, but lived most of their adult lives in Austin. Both men spelled their name "Engbloom."

Rudolph and Theodore as children, an enlargement from a family picture

Theodore, the oldest, married a local farmer's daughter, Lillian Adeline Anderson. They had three children: Maydell (b. 1914), Laverne Aileen (1917-2008) and Mary Frances (1926-1982).

Theodore's WW I draft card said he was tall, of medium build, with black hair and brown eyes. At the time he registered, he was 26 years old and working as a farmer.

 Theodore's draft signature

By the 1940s Theodore was working as a fireman in the Austin City Electric Department. He died at age 74 of an aortic rupture, complicated by atherosclerosis.

Theodore as a young man, date unknown.

From *Swedes in Texas*, 1918:

F. T. ENGBLOM was born in Austin, Texas, in 1890. His father is Andrew Engblom in Lund. The son grew up in his parents' home. He attended Trinity College for some time. In 1913 he married Lillian Anderson, daughter of A. F. Anderson in New Sweden. She was born in 1892 in New Sweden and has lived with her parents ever since.

The Engbloms live on A.F. Anderson's homestead and belong to the Lutheran Church in New Sweden. Their small daughter, Maydell Adeline, is a ray of sunshine in the home. She was born in 1914. Engblom is a progressive farmer, and we predict that he has a bright future ahead of him.

Theodore and Lillian Engbloom, wedding photograph, 1913.

The Engblooms (circa 1915). Lillian is just visible behind the car at the front. To the left are Rudolph, then Ella (holding Maydell) and Theodore on the right.

Rudolph was a cotton farmer as a young man. Eventually he left farming and worked as a taxicab dispatcher and maintenance man in Austin. His draft card said he was of medium build with brown eyes and light brown hair. For some reason, his height was omitted. When he registered, he was already married to Ivy Eve Ruth Chiles.

REGISTRATION CARD.

Rudolph and Ruth had three children: Nellie (b. 1919), Virginia (b 1920), and Ralph Lorentz (1921-1944). Rudolph's daughter Nellie played with Mama when they were children. Ruth Engblom worked as a saleswoman and window dresser in department stores.

Rudolph died at 74, from lung cancer. Ruth died in 1992. Rudolph and Ruth are buried in the Austin Memorial Park Cemetery.

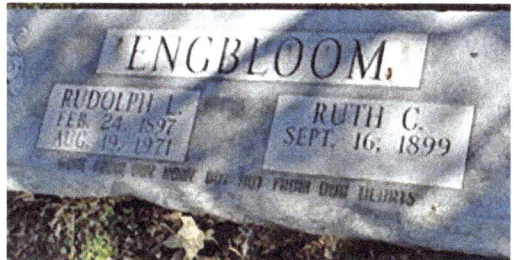

# The Westling family

Jonas Westling was born in 1828 in Varnola parish, Västergötland, Sweden. Västergötland is a southwestern Swedish province, bordering Östergötland and Småland. Lake Vättern is on the east side, and the province includes fertile plains, forested hills, and rivers.

Some of the information I have on the Westlings came from Chuck Carlson, who has researched the family more thoroughly. Chuck's great grandmother and my great grandmother were both daughters of Jonas. Chuck was able to correct some of the errors I initially made in the Westling family tree.

Jonas married Johanna Sophia Peterson and had ten children, of whom I know nine names:

129

Josephine Charlotte (Lotten) 1855-1935, my great grandmother, died age 80.
Johan Albert 1859-1893, died age 34.
Gerhard Theodore 1860-1930, died age 70.
Carl Emil 1862-1864, died age 2.
Conrad Theofil 1864-1935, died age 71.
Esther Amalia 1865-1940, died age 75.
Anna Sophia 1867-1955, died age 88, Chuck's great-grandmother.
Hilda Dorthea 1869-1964, died age 95.
Theresia (no birth or death date)

Jonas Americanized his name to "John," but it was sometimes recorded as Johan. Before he moved to America, he changed his last name to Westling. His brother Anders did the same. I am not sure why they chose that particular name. Chuck thinks it might be because they lived in the western part of Sweden. A number of Swedes took this name after about 1900, when family names in Sweden became more fixed in the style of other European nations. The most famous Westling today is probably Daniel Westling, who married the Swedish Crown Princess. He was the princess' personal fitness trainer.

John Westling's brother Anders Westling was two years older. Their father was Anders Christoffersson. Anders Westling and his wife Elen Johannson had three children: Matilda, Anna and Oscar.

Jonas came from Sweden in 1881 with his family. He was fifty-three years old. They first arrived in Bridgeport, Connecticut and then moved to Texas, where Jonas' brother Anders and one of Jonas' sons were already settled. He rented land near New Sweden, and his wife and children soon followed. Chuck told me that Jonas bought land in Texas before actually moving there. The U.S. Federal Census Non-Population Schedule shows John as a farm owner in New Sweden, Travis County, in 1880, a year before he immigrated.

Bridgeport was a target city for many European immigrants in the late 1800s because it was a big manufacturing center.

Factories in the city made sewing machines, pianos, rifles, corsets and a multitude of other essential products. There were many factory jobs for immigrants who had little English and no specialized job skills.

By letter, Jonas persuaded some of his Swedish friends in Bridgeport to come and join him in Texas. Two of these friends were brothers, Carl and Fred Bergman. The brothers lived with the Westling family for a while, and then bought land near the Westling property in Lund. They wrote regular letters to their sisters in Sweden for many years. The sisters kept all the letters, which were eventually published. They give a remarkable look at what life must have been like for the Westlings, Engbloms and Carlsons. Some of these letters are translated in Larry Scott's book, *The Swedish Texans*, and are worth a read. The brothers made mention of American women, whom they considered too small and delicate when compared to Swedes. Also, they thought American women were bad cooks.

John Westling (from *Swedes in Texas*)

From *Swedes in Texas*, 1918:

JOHN WESTLING emigrated with his family in 1881 and came to the United States. He left his family in Bridgeport, Conn., and travelled alone to New Sweden, Texas, where he had a brother, Anders Westling, and a son. After having seen Texas, he decided to make his home there, and in the following year he went to bring his family. Mr. Westling leased land in New Sweden community for a few years, but in 1889 he bought land near Lund. John Westling was born in Varnola parish, Västergötland, in 1828. He married Johanna Sophia Peterson who was born in 1834 in Vikingstad parish, the district of Linköping. Their marriage was blessed with ten children, of whom seven are still living: Lotten, Esther, Anna, Hilda, Theresia, Gerhard, and Conrad. Mrs. Westling died in 1894, and Mr. Westling, 1914. When they came to Texas, they joined the Lutheran congrega-tion in New Sweden, but after they moved to Lund, they joined the Lutheran congregation there. After his wife died, Mr. Westling lived with his daughter and son-in-law, A. Engblom, in Lund. Mr. West-ling got a good education. In Sweden he was inspector at several large manors and when he arrived in this country, he was known as "Inspector Westling.

The job of "Inspector" meant John was a supervisor and managed manorial activities. These might have included farming, lumbering, smelting, or mining. It was the kind of job that required at least two more years of education past elementary school, which ended at $8^{th}$ grade. Chuck told me that Jonas attended one of the agricultural schools in Sweden, and was able to send me a photo-graph of Jonas' 1852 certificate from agricultural school. He attended Sjogestad Agriculture School, and the certificate is dated 22 Oct 1852. Jonas was twenty-four years old. Sjogestad is a tiny town east of Lake Vättern, in Östergötland. The agricultural school Jonas attended is no longer in existence.

I could not translate some of the words in the document, with an on-line translator. Some words are actually not Swedish, but Icelandic or Norwegian, and may not be commonly used in modern Swedish. This is the gist of it, as accurately as I could manage:

Agriculture Apprentice J. Westling has been a resident of this region and has a square (official?) degree. He was an employee when he received the following insights (evaluations? grades?) at the Headquarters of Land Use and Stockraising.

Accurate Bookkeeping and Writing: *Good.*

Diligence *Credit*
Behavior *Credit*
Working Skills *Good*

Any teacher or student knows that "Credit" means a passing grade. "Good" is something better than barely passing. It looks like his diligence and behavior were not as satisfactory as they could have been. I wonder what he did, or failed to do, to impress his teachers.

The 1910 census shows that Andrew Engblom, Lotten, Theodore, Rudolph and John Westling were living in Travis County, Texas. Ella is not listed, as she was attending the Lutheran College in Round Rock.

Mama wrote that her great-grandfather Jonas Westling was a trader for at least part of his life in Sweden. He traveled to northern Sweden and traded with the Sami people, also called Lapps or Laplanders. Sometimes he took his children with him on those trips. Lotten told Mama that she had seen herds of reindeer and the northern lights. On some of his trips around southern Sweden they traveled by boat, on the Göta Canal that crosses Östergötland.

Jonas died in 1914 Williamson County, Texas, and was buried in the Lund cemetery.

When I began researching the Carlsons, I did not intend to include my grandmother Ella's family. But once I got started, I found myself taking side trips into the lives of the Engbloms and Westlings. I decided that my mother would have liked having her mother's people incorporated into this work. Mama adored her maternal grandparents, Anders and Lotten Engblom. She had fond memories of her uncles Theodore and Rudolph, and their wives and children.

I love the romantic story of Anders and Lotten, how they met on a ship bound for America and Lotten's willingness to wait for Anders until he saved enough money to marry. Anders' life history is fascinating. He was truly a self-made man, and the perfect example of a hardworking, successful American immigrant.

Until I researched Lotten Engblom's parents, I had never even heard her father's name. In the process of discovering more about the Westlings, I learned much more about the lives of nineteenth century Swedes and the difficulties they faced. The Westlings were every bit as interesting and remarkable as were the Carlsons.

A few of Lotten's tales about her childhood have been passed along for five generations now. I wish I could have heard from her own lips about traveling on the Gota Canal with her father Jonas, seeing the northern lights, and meeting Sami people and their reindeer. I hope that when my descendants and relatives read this book, they also will appreciate the rich and varied lives of our Scandinavian ancestors.

I have not tried to put my sources into any particular scholarly citation format. The information provided should be enough for an interested reader to locate the references.

Websites with Historical Information

*History of Sweden*, by the Swedish Institute, a publicly funded Swedish nonprofit organization.
https://sweden.se/society/history-of-sweden/

*Social Structure and Social Mobility in Southern Sweden 1751-1894*, paper presented at the SSHA-meeting in St Louis 24-27 October 2002 Session B 03, Social mobility in the past. John Adler and Patrick Svensson.
http://web.iaincirebon.ac.id/ebook/moon/SocialMatters/ELC2002-08.pdf

*The Cultural Landscape South of Lake Boren,* Östergötland, *Sweden*, by Emma Hagstrom. An INTERREG Project. 2004.
http://centrostudinatura.it/public2/documenti/288-19161.pdf

*Current status of the hermit beetle (Osmoderma eremita) in Jonkoping County* by Ellen Flygare. Degree project in Biology, including information on parts of Jonkoping County, land usage, habitat fragmentation and history.
http://www.ibg.uu.se/digitalAssets/164/164785_3flygare-ellen-arbete.pdf

*Report on the Swedish Exposition at the Chicago World's Fair, 1893.*
Lots of information on Swedish economy and agriculture.
http://archive.org/stream/worldscolumbiane00whit/worldscolumbiane00whit_djvu.txt

Digital Gateway to Texas History, *Handbook of Texas.*
Maintained by the Texas State Historical Society.
http://www.tshaonline.org/handbook/online

*Texas History Timeline (Key Events in Early Texas)*
       http://www.lsjunction.com/events/events.htm
Site maintained by Lone Star Junction, part of the Texas State
Historical Society.

Online Texas history site called Lonestar Genealogy.
http://www.lonestargenealogy.com/courses/texas/swedishset.html

University of North Texas website, Beyond the Bytes, The Portal
to Texas History.
http://education.texashistory.unt.edu/news/Newsletters/archive
/2012May.html

*The 1918 Influenza Epidemic,* by Marilyn Dunnahoo McLeod for
MOCHA (Manchaca Onion Creek Historical Association).
http://www.mochaonline.org/InfluenzaFullArticle.pdf

*Midwifery in American Institutes of Higher Education: Women's
Work,*
*Vocations and the 21st Century,* by Mary C. Brucker.
http://forumonpublicpolicy.com/summer09/archivesummer09/
brucker.pdf

Online magazine, Midwifery Today, *The History of Midwifery
and Childbirth in America: A Time Line.* by Adrian E. Feldhusen,
Midwife. http://www.midwiferytoday.com/articles/timeline.asp

*The UFO Airships of 1896 – 1897,* by Steven A. Arts. 2004.
http://www.weeklyuniverse.com/2004/airships.htm

*Historic Resource Survey of Northeast Travis County* (Bound by SH130, US 290 North and East County Lines). Prepared by: Hicks & Company, Austin, Texas. Hannah Vaughan, MSAS, Principal Investigator. Prepared for The Travis County Historical Commission. This is a survey of historical buildings. http://www.co.travis.tx.us/historical_commission/pdfs/ne_tc_full_report.pdf

*Texas Escapes*, an online magazine, source of old photographs and information on ghost towns, Texas history, etc. http://www.texasescapes.com/Cotton/Texas-Cotton-Scenes.htm

Williamson County Historical Commission website: http://www.williamson-county-historical-commission.org/Round_rock/Round_Rock_Texas_in_williamson_county.htm

Websites dealing specifically with Swedish Immigration:

Swedish/English dictionary and terms for genealogical research. http://www.algonet.se/~hogman/dictionary_genealogy.htm

*Swedish American Historical Quarterly* http://swedishamericanhist.org/publications/index.html

Swedish Immigrant Institute, information about immigrants to America from Smaland. http://www.utvandrarnashus.se/eng/

*The Swedish Migrants to Texas*, by Magnus Morner, Swedish-American Historical Quarterly (North Oak University) April 1987, v 38, no. 2.

*Swedish American Genealogy and Local History: Selected Titles at the Library of Congress.* Compiled and Annotated by Lee V. Douglas
http://www.loc.gov/rr/genealogy/bib_guid/swedish.pdf

Swedish Genetics: Abstracts and Summaries
http://www.khazaria.com/genetics/swedes.html

Swedish Council of America
http://www.swedishcouncil.org

Ancestors and Family of Barry, Ojerholm and Smith. Private site with information on the Ojerholms.
http://www.ojerholm.com/aqwg03.htm

*The Lay of Per Svensson: Competing Propaganda Campaigns in 19th Century Swedish Emigration.*
http://williamemery.wordpress.com/2013/06/07/the-lay-of-per-svensson-competing-propaganda-campaigns-in-19th-century-swedish-emigration/

Hans Högman's Genealogy and History Site, *The Emigration from Sweden to the United States*, and other useful articles, including information on genealogical research.
http://www.algonet.se/~hogman/swedish_emigration_to_usa.htm

Story of Hardin House, a boarding house in Austin, on Rio Grande St, near where Ellen Blomquist's boarding house was located.
http://www.hardinhouse.com/web222/history/default.asp

Augustana College (Illinois) website for the Swenson Swedish Immigration Research Center.

https://www.augustana.edu/general-information/swenson-center-/swedish-american-immigration-history

Electronic Books:

*Swedes in Texas in words and pictures, 1918.* Published by J. M. Ojerholm.

*An Economic History of Sweden* by Lars Magnusson, 2000.

*The Nobilities of Europe*, edited by Marquis de Ruvigny, 1909.

*Report on Forestry in Sweden to the United States Senate, 1900*, by General Christopher Columbus Andrews, U. S. minister at Stockholm.

*Peasantry to Capitalism: Western Östergötland in the Nineteenth Century,* by Göran Hoppe.

*Norway and Sweden: Handbook for Travelers* by Kim Baedeker, 1885.

*American Swedish 73*, edited by Leif Sjoberg, for the American Swedish Historical Foundation.

*The Finnish Economy 1860-1985*, by Riita Hjerppe, 1999.

Print Books:

*Story of the 1900 Galveston Hurricane*, edited by Nathan Green, 1900.

*Anna's Journey, a Story of Early Swedish Immigrants to Texas.* by Elroy Haverlah, 2014.

*Elgin, Etc., Stories of Elgin, Texas*, by Elgin Historical Society, 2008.

*Images of America: Elgin.* by Sydna Arbuckle and Judy Davis. 2012.

*A History of Elgin, Texas 1872-1972*, by Elgin Historical Society, 1972.

*The Swedish Texans*, by Larry Scott, 1990.

*A Folk Divided: Homeland Swedes and Swedish Americans 1840-1940,* by H. Arnold Barton, 1994.

# Carlson Family Lineage

Carl August Carlson (1849-1915) m. Matilda Person (1850-1903)
> Children:
1. Carl Werner (1874-1966)
2. Anna Gunilla (1876-1972)
3. Carl Arvid (1879-1959)
4. Jennie Augusta (1880-1923)
5. Ellen Matilda (1882-1964)
6. August Richard (1885-1973)
7. Oscar Ivar (1890-1967)
8. Nina Elvira (1896-1911)
9. Erik (1896o1898?)

1. Verner (1874-1966) m Frances Henson Tipton (1888-1969)
> Children:
> Carl Verner Carlson Jr. (1925-2002)
> John Elmer Carlson (1928-1976)

2. Annie (1876-1972) no marriage

3. Arvid (1879-1959) m. Amelia Johnson (1888-1974)
> Children:
> Hildred Stotts 1909-2000
> Helen Boettcher 1910-2000
> Arvie Carl 1912- 2000
> Evelyn 1915-1934
> Roland 1918-1997

4. Jennie (1880-1923) no marriage

5. Ellen (1882-1964) m. Carl Blomquist (1882-1919)
> Children:
> Verno (1911-1999)
> Leverne (1915-2002)

Chester (1909-1980)
Frances Mathilda (Simon) (1907-1984)
Anna Genevieve (Pugh) (1918 –)

6. Richard (1885-1973) m. Iona Lohman (1919-2001)
    Children:
    Richard William Carlson (1928-2014)
    Charles August Carlson (1947-)

7. Oscar (1890-1967) m. Ella Engblom (1889-1930)
    Children:
    Charlotte Rosebell (1918-2004)

Ella Engblom's Family Lineage:

Jonas Westling (1828-1914) m Johanna Sophia Peterson (1834-1894)
    Children:
    Josephine Charlotte (1855-1935), Ella's mother
    Johan Albert (1859-1893)
    Gerhard Theodore (1860-1930)
    Carl Emil (1862-1864)
    Conrad Theofil 1864-1935)
    Esther Amalia (1865-1940)
    Anna Sophia (1867-1955)
    Hilda Dorthea (1869-1964)
    Theresia (no dates)

Anders Engblom (1853-1925) m Josephine Charlotte Westling (1855-1935)
    Children:
    Ella Engblom (1889-1930) m Oscar Carlson
    Frank Theodore Engblom (1891-1965) m Lillian Anderson
    Rudolph Lorentz Engblom (1897-1971) m Ivy Eve Ruth
        Chiles

www.ingramcontent.com/pod-product-compliance
Lightning Source LLC
Chambersburg PA
CBHW050844270326
41930CB00020B/3464